ENDORSEMENTS

"The ideas in *The Non-Obvious Guide to Emotional Intelligence* helped move us in less than a year from a mediocre company to a rapidly growing, highly profitable enterprise. Kerry's techniques are simple, effective, easily implemented, and readily understood by everyone in our organization."

George E. Garrison, PhD, President & CEO, SantoLubes

"This book gave me concrete ways to identify level-headed problem-solvers for my team. More importantly, it provides the tools to train and motivate them as loyal, servant leaders—a hallmark of Southwest Airlines' Culture. If you're interested in creating stronger, more successful teams in your company, this book is for you!"

Jason Van Eaton, Senior Vice President, Governmental Affairs and Real Estate, Southwest Airlines

"*The Non-Obvious Guide to Emotional Intelligence* is a book every CEO should read. Kerry Goyette provides a useful overview of the topic with excellent academic research references. She clearly explains how each element of emotional intelligence can be usefully applied by leaders and managers in order to make themselves and their workforce better equipped to make good decisions."

Dr. Rita Kirk, Altshuler Distinguished Professor of Corporate Communications & Public Affairs, Southern Methodist University

"Kerry Goyette takes EQ to the next level. She shows how to move from me EQ to we EQ, and then helps put it into practice. After reading *The Non-Obvious Guide to Emotional Intelligence*, you will learn how your environment can help or hurt you, and why intrinsic motivation can be the most powerful force of all. Get this book. You'll be a better leader for it."

Phil West, Chair, Steptoe & Johnson LLP

"If being an agile leader that gets the most from their organization is important to you, invest in this book! Goyette quickly cuts to the heart of issues facing leaders and managers of people. What motivates staff, how to create a more productive environment, and learning that your "gut" is not always right are all part of this insightful book."

Cris Burnam, President, StorageMart

"Anyone interested in becoming a better leader should read *The Non-Obvious Guide to Emotional Intelligence*. In today's world, EQ is one of the most important strengths of a professional. Goyette's a gifted writer who turns the science of EQ into something digestible."

John Hall, Author of Top of Mind and Co-founder of Calendar.com

"The biggest shift in leadership since the 7 Habits."

Keri Tipton, CEO, Bucket Media, Inc.

"As the director of a dynamic not-for-profit, I know how essential emotional intelligence is today for quick, high-impact decision-making. Goyette is a helpful guide to obtaining this crucial leadership skill in a hurry. Highly recommended!"

Jeremy Brown, Executive Director, Ragtag Film Society

"If you believe that "soft" people skills are as important to management success as "hard", technical skills then you must read this book! Goyette's approach to the science of people skills is both compelling and effective. Front line supervisors and CEOs alike will benefit from this book's lessons."

Kate Hampford Donahue, President & CEO, Hampford Research, Inc.

"This book is a gift to leaders who understand that being successful in today's environment requires additional tools, but don't know how to articulate or understand what they're missing. Goyette explains that it's emotional intelligence, in a book that provides the reader a practical, entertaining, and insightful guide into the science behind emotional intelligence and provides ways to successfully harness it."

Jodie Kelley, Senior Vice President & General Counsel, BSA | The Software Alliance

"Whether you're an executive in the C-Suite focused on winning the race for talent or a line worker wondering how to keep a robot from taking his job, *The Non-Obvious Guide to Emotional Intelligence* is a must-read. I'd recommend getting a copy for your employees, managers, spouse, and kids too!"

Ira S Wolfe, Chief Googlization Officer, Success Performance Solutions; Author, Recruiting in the Age of Googlization

"It's important to note that Kerry has credentials and a wealth of experience in the area of human performance, but what makes her especially unique is that she can take a take such a complicated topic, one that most people would drone on about, and make it interesting, easy to understand, and simple to apply. You'll see benefits in your life before you finish the first chapter."

Doug Hanson, Motivational Speaker / Humorist / Author

"A fabulous book in its capacity to clearly articulate the 'potholes' that continue to derail us, our work communities, and our work from their full potential in the digital age. *The Non-Obvious Guide to Emotional Intelligence* roadmap is essential to driving forward in today's work world and in the flourishing of our companies."

Sharon Perry, Founder/CEO of iBexEd

"When leaders clearly understand the "why" behind how we lead, the "why" behind how our team follows, and the brain science behind it all, we can build more effective environments and systems for our team to be better together. If you are a growth-oriented leader, you don't want to miss the rich insights in Kerry's newest book."

Lisa Nichols, Co-founder & CEO, Technology Partners

"A fresh look at emotional intelligence and turning the EQ leadership equation from me to we! Kerry's use of real life stories, neuroscience, and her professional experiences helped me not only engage in the book, but apply it to how I lead others."

Eujin Ahn, Manager Organizational Development, Fresenius Kabi USA

"Kerry understands how foundational trust and safety are to all relationships even in the workplace. This book emphasizes the necessity of taking EQ beyond navel gazing and toward connection and purpose."

Mike Sense, Founder & Director, Global Counseling Network

"As long as you're working with people, you'll be working with their emotions. This book is a manual to what's going on inside the minds and hearts of the people you work alongside."

David Burkus, Author of Friend of a Friend

"This is a fun and engaging read that gives practical advice on improving performance through building leadership capacity toward emotional intelligence. The book balances that practical advice with recent scientific data to support its application."

Darrin Murriner, Co-founder & CEO, Cloverleaf

The **NON-OBVIOUS
GUIDE TO**

Emotional
Intelligence

(You Can Actually Use)

By **KERRY GOYETTE**

IDEAPRESS
PUBLISHING

IDEAPRESS
PUBLISHING

Published in the United States by Ideapress Publishing.

IDEAPRESS PUBLISHING | WWW.IDEAPRESSPUBLISHING.COM

All trademarks are the property of their respective companies.

COVER DESIGN BY JOCELYN MANDRYK

Cataloging-in-Publication Data is on file with the Library of Congress.

ISBN: 978-1-940858-91-3

PROUDLY PRINTED IN THE USA

SPECIAL SALES

Ideapress Books are available at a special discount for bulk purchases, for sales promotions and premiums, or for use in corporate training programs. Special editions, including personalized covers, a custom foreword, corporate imprints, and bonus content are also available.

Non-Obvious® is a registered trademark of the Influential Marketing Group.

DEDICATION

To my husband Joe, who still knows how
to make me laugh, and is always up for being
my next lab experiment.

To Bailey, Megan, Wesley, and Jana.
You are my source of inspiration and motivation.
Your love and support means more than you know.

To my mom and dad.
Thank you for always being there for me.

Read this book to learn why emotional intelligence (EQ) really matters and how to use EQ to connect with people, earn more money, and help your business grow. If you want to better understand yourself, others, and the world around you, this book will help you do it.

Contents /

v   **What Will You Learn?**

vii **Introduction**

PART ONE – DECISION-MAKING

Chapter 1

01 **Where Does Empathy Start?**
 → Why Leaders Wear Sweaters - How to Practice Empathy
 → Get Over Yourself - the Biggest Mistake People Make with EQ
 → What Is Holistic Emotional Intelligence?
 → Case Study: When *We* Works for Everyone
 → The Three Elements of Change
 → How to Put The Three Elements of Change to Work

Chapter 2

21 **Fear, Threats, And The Way Our Brains Perceive Our Environments**
 → Don't Fight Your Brain, Embrace It
 → The "Fight-or-Flight" Response
 → The Sad Rise of Blame-Shifting
 → Why We Tend to Focus on the Negative
 → How to Evaluate Your Decision-Making

Chapter 3

47 **How Courage Drives Emotional Intelligence**

→ How to Create a Better Environment

→ Getting to the Root: How to Ask Courageous Questions

→ Start With Clearly Identifying the Threats

→ Case Study: Why No Man Is an Island (Not Even You, Patrick)

→ How to Use Pauses to Strategically Overcome Fear

→ Integrating the Elements of EQ

PART TWO – AGILITY

Chapter 4

75 **How To Recognize Your Environment**

→ VUCA is the New Four Letter Word

→ The Difference Between Problems and Dilemmas

→ Case Study

→ The Real Secret to Managing VUCA

Chapter 5

91 **How To Increase Your Agility**

→ The EQ³ Advantage

→ Case Study: How to Drive Real Change

→ Four Tips to Navigate the (Mental) Agility Course

→ The Importance of Agility

→ How to Improve Your Agility

PART THREE – RELATIONSHIPS

Chapter 6

109 **Understanding Team Dysfunction**

→ How We Derail Ourselves from Success

→ The Six Common Derailers

→ We're Not as Self-Aware as We Think

→ How to Recognize Derailers in Others

→ Case Study: Meeting the Challenge of Identifying Your Derailers

→ The Importance of Being Self-Aware

→ How to Adopt a Growth Mindset

→ How to Manage and Overcome Your Derailers

Chapter 7

143 **How To Motivate Your Team (And Yourself)**

→ What Not to Do: Compliance and "The Carrot & The Stick"

→ Why the Workplace Isn't Like a Carnival Game

→ Intrinsic vs. Extrinsic Motivation

→ Why Smart Companies Don't Base Compensation on Employee Goals

→ The Six Drivers of Intrinsic Motivation

→ How to Drive Intrinsic Motivation among Your Team

Chapter 8

167 **Take Motivation From *Me* To *We* To *Why***

→ How to Provide Recognition

→ How to Deliver More Clarity

→ How to Empower Your Team

→ How to Collaborate and Coach

→ How to Operate with Transparency and Be Fair

→ The Best Leaders are Meaning Makers

187 **Conclusion**

191 **Endnotes**

201 **Index**

Is This Guide for You?

If you picked up this book, you are not a dummy.

Many business guides treat you like an idiot. Some even say so on the cover. This is not one of those books.

The Non-Obvious Guides all focus on sharing advice that you haven't heard before. The first time I met Kerry (over a coffee, of course!), I knew she was the perfect choice to write our guide on one of the hottest topics in leadership over the past decade–emotional intelligence. If you want to better understand and inspire the people around you, I guarantee this book will help you do it.

Like all of our guides, this one is down-to-earth and highly actionable. It is indeed the next best thing to having coffee with Kerry herself, which I also recommend if you ever get the chance.

Rohit Bhargava
Founder, *Non-Obvious Guides*

How to Read This Book

Throughout this book, you will find links to helpful guides and resources online.

DOWNLOAD LINK:
http://www.thinkaperio.com/eq3book

Referenced in the book, you will also see these symbols which refer to content that will further your learning.

FOLLOW THE ICONS:

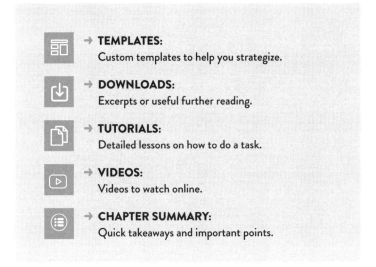

TEMPLATES:
Custom templates to help you strategize.

DOWNLOADS:
Excerpts or useful further reading.

TUTORIALS:
Detailed lessons on how to do a task.

VIDEOS:
Videos to watch online.

CHAPTER SUMMARY:
Quick takeaways and important points.

In this book, you will learn how to...

→ Improve your decision-making when it matters most.

→ Navigate change and better manage disruption.

→ Avoid making decisions driven by your brain's "fight-or-flight" mode.

→ Trace problems to their roots so they can be solved more easily.

→ Understand why the old "carrot & stick" style of motivation no longer works.

→ Identify the "derailers" that may be holding you back.

→ Be agile and thrive in today's chaotic environments.

→ Motivate your employees in a way that drives loyalty.

Introduction

It's August 1981: Major League Baseball is back in full swing, Indiana Jones valiantly saved the Ark of the Covenant, and *Time* magazine declares that they have discovered the best ice cream, not just in America, but in the world. While you could watch America's beloved pastime and Jones' adventures across the world, this renowned ice cream could only be enjoyed in one spot: a refurbished gas station in Vermont.

Unfortunately, despite being declared the best ice cream in the world, the guys running the shop were running it into the ground. With both of their life savings invested, a bank loan to repay, and their pride on the line, they needed to start turning a profit. Being open 16 hours a day, 7 days a week, and dishing out one-of-a-kind flavors just wasn't enough. I guess you could say that Ben and Jerry didn't excel at the management side of their business.

"We were really good at creating an atmosphere in the shop that was welcoming and fun, less than excellent at hiring people, at supervising people," says Jerry Greenfield. "And most of all, we were really bad at portion control."[1]

See, in almost every other restaurant business, explains Ben Cohen, the portions are controlled in the kitchen, out of the sight of the customer.

But with ice cream?

"You know, when you scoop out a nice, big scoop for a customer, you get this beautiful smile and really warm response," Jerry says. "And it's really positive reinforcement for over-scooping. And, you know, Ben and I, we wanted to make people happy."

Ben and Jerry valued the instantaneous gratification of happy customers over their bottom line. And this was becoming a growing concern for the sustainability of their scoops.

So just what were these two ice cream makers to do? Their real secret ingredient came down to two words that you are probably already familiar with.

WHAT'S SO NON-OBVIOUS ABOUT EQ?

We've all heard the term "emotional intelligence"(also referred to as "EQ")—so much so that it's now a buzzword. We know it's listed on job descriptions and cited as an attribute to cultivate in young people.

Emotional intelligence has become a crucial part of what we look for in coworkers, bosses, employees, children, and even ourselves.

But when we really break it down, how many of us can identify the elements that make up this term?

Most of the ink that's been spilled on emotional intelligence leans toward a version of EQ that focuses on the individual. It goes something like this: be nicer to coworkers and you build empathy; more empathy means people like you more, which leads to you being a more successful leader. Now, don't get me wrong, empathy is important, of course.

If you focus *only* on empathy, you're missing crucial ways to be emotionally intelligent.

The questions we need to foreground in the conversation are not just about *me*—they're about *we* and *why*.

Emotionally intelligent leaders move beyond *me*, through *we*, and into *why*.

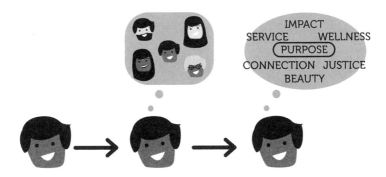

In this book, we'll discuss things like: How can we leverage emotional intelligence for the good of the whole? That's the whole group you're in or, as a leader, your whole organization. This means we address the environment. Which raises the question: How do highly emotionally intelligent teams not just survive, but thrive, in their environment? And: What can the newest brain science teach us about emotionally intelligent decision-making?

Often EQ is thought to be all about examining the individual or oneself—*my* emotions, *my* feelings, *my* approach to others.

Think of this book's approach as emotional intelligence cubed—or EQ³. It asks each of us to look not only at the self, but also at relationships and the environment. These three pieces—self, relationship, and environment—are crucial to becoming a more emotionally intelligent leader.

EQ³ = self + relationships + environment

WHY DOES EMOTIONAL INTELLIGENCE MATTER?

If robots are all set to take over, can emotional intelligence really save us? Well, before you write off the value of real people, consider these facts:

→ 90% of top performers have a higher level of emotional intelligence.[2]

→ Emotional intelligence accounts for 90% of career advancements when IQ and technical skills are roughly similar.[3]

→ Your emotional intelligence is responsible for over half of your job performance (fifty-eight percent, to be exact).[4]

→ People with high emotional intelligence make $29,000 more, on average, than their counterparts.[5]

→ A recent study from the Carnegie Institute demonstrated that 85% of your financial success was due to skills in "human engineering," personality, and ability to communicate, negotiate, and lead. Only 15% of your financial success, it turned out, was due to technical ability.[6]

→ According to the work of Nobel Prize–winning psychologist Daniel Kahneman, people would rather do business with a person they like and trust than someone they don't, even if the person they don't is offering a better product at a lower price.[7]

So what am I saying? That a high EQ will make you perform better, earn you more money, and help your business grow? Well... Yes.

And perhaps you've heard promises like that before in books that seem like this one. But the difference with this guide is that we move beyond the surface-level stuff. We talk about the *me* and then go further—we go into *we* and then to *why*. We talk about how the brain works and why that matters to you and your team. You need this *why* if you're going to succeed. Because here's one thing I'll bet you already know: if you're going to make a *permanent* change, whether it's breaking an old habit or implementing a new way of working, you need to drill down to the why. And you need to think about how to set the environment up for your and your team's success.

To see how this works in real life, let's go back to the story of Ben and Jerry. When their fledgling ice cream shop started struggling, they asked *why*. They knew that scooping big cones of delicious, creamy goodness made them happy—portion size be damned. The environment and the very *design* of the ice cream shop was set up to give them a little rush when they saw that customer smile. But this was focused entirely on them.

Asking *why* is the first step of the EQ³ approach. You have to be willing to drill down and figure out what about the environment and what about the brain is positioning you to behave a certain way.

Ben and Jerry were popular but not yet successful until asking *why* started a chain reaction that led them to a solution. They noticed their *me* tendencies and how that fit into the *we* pattern of the shop. If they were going to find success, they would have to reimagine how they could deliver their delicious product.

What did they do next? It would be hard to succeed with the traditional environment where customers watch employees scoop their treats. So they changed their model drastically in a way you probably already know all too well, if you look inside your freezer at home.

WHY I WROTE THIS BOOK

When I travel around the world to work with individuals and teams at companies, it's often for one or more of the following reasons:

- → They're in the middle of a great period of change;
- → A mistake has just been made; or
- → Something just isn't working.

Sometimes, our instinct when things get rocky is to just try and push through. Hold on, and this too shall pass.

It's probably true—it will pass—but at what cost?

My goal for writing this book is ideally to reach *you* before you get into that rocky zone. If you're already there, then I am here to help you navigate it and better adapt to the next challenge.

Part of what makes my approach to emotional intelligence unique is that I work with the latest in social science research.

Emotions stem from the deepest, oldest part of our brain—the limbic center. In terms of the brain, the source of emotions is very different from the source of reason.

My work takes into account the very nature of the brain because I believe if we can't understand the basics of how our brain works, then it's nearly impossible to work *with* it. Daniel Goleman's notion of emotional intelligence and the five associated skills were critical in the early success of my consulting business.[8] They provided a practical framework to guide leader development.

Having used EQ now for two decades, I still find new ways to apply its concepts. This book is my attempt to marry emotional intelligence with newer discoveries and applications of brain science that have come to light since EQ's original publication, without the need for you to become a neuroscience researcher yourself. These new combinations have challenged my thinking and changed the way I lead, partner, and serve. Through this book, I want to share some non-obvious discoveries and how the three frameworks of environment, relationships, and self have created for me an EQ^3 advantage.

There are three parts to this book. Each part focuses on one of three key areas: decision-making, agility, and relationships. The first part includes an approachable and useful dive into the brain science behind EQ; the second touches quite a bit on the environment; and the third has to do with motivation and how to rethink your approach. In every chapter, we talk about the *me,* the *we,* and the *why.* In every chapter, you learn how you can move from *me* through *we* and into *why*.

However you choose to use this book, my goal is for you to walk away with a better understanding of yourself, others, and the world around you. And for you to be able to do something with that understanding.

PINT-SIZE PARADISE

And as for Ben and Jerry? They understood their *me* as it connected to *we*. And then they saw how the environment—the ice cream shop setup incentivized scooping big portions—was impacting their individual behavior and their collective sales. At the same time, they knew they didn't want to change those big scoops—it was the aspect of their work that had given them joy, not to mention a story in *Time* magazine.

So what *did* they do? They didn't wait for the environment to change. They changed it for themselves. They adapted and innovated. They began to package their ice cream into pints and started selling it beyond the walls of their shop. In other words, they addressed the me, the we, and the environment.

HOW APPLYING EQ³ SAVED
BEN & JERRY'S BUSINESS STRATEGY

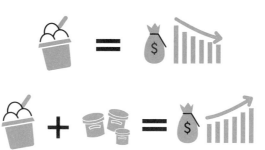

Now, you might be asking: what does this adaptation have to do with Ben and Jerry's emotions? In other words: how is *that* emotional intelligence? This is where EQ[3] enters the picture:

Emotional intelligence is not simply about understanding emotions or emoting more. It is the *intelligent use of emotion* to understand a situation and make better decisions.

After all, a pint is a pint, no more, no less. By 1987, Ben and Jerry had built a $30 million empire. To me, this triumph conveys the idea that EQ is more than emotional skills. EQ is also a dance between the mind and matter, between the subjective experience of our internal world and the objective reality with which it tries to cope. When

I take this broader view of EQ, factoring in our mental hardwiring and environmental chaos, what I call EQ^3, I find new levers to move my world.

In the midst of my research into Ben and Jerry, I discovered that they not only used their abundant emotional intelligence to run their ice cream empire, but they advocated for emotional intelligence by having partnered, in 2016, with a local college to create courses in which their employees can build EQ and other skills.[9] If those two happy, ice-cream-loving guys aren't the faces of EQ, I don't know who is.

In addition to their shelf in your grocer's freezer, Ben and Jerry still have their ice cream shop—there are locations all around the world. And you know what? The last time I was at a Ben & Jerry's ice cream shop, the scoops were still big.

PART ONE
Decision-Making

CHAPTER 1

Where Does Empathy Start?

Have you seen the award-winning documentary about TV icon Fred Rogers, titled *Won't You Be My Neighbor?*[10] I have—Mr. Rogers was a token of my childhood—and one scene struck me as particularly interesting. In it, Mr. Rogers sits in a classroom full of children he had never met before, preparing for one of his famous puppet shows. As he unpacks his puppets, Mr. Rogers notices the silence and how closely the children are watching him.

The children had been waiting, Mr. Rogers says, to see what he would do.

Mr. Rogers pulls out a puppet.

A boy raises his hand. He declares his stuffed dog's ear came off in the washing machine.

And there was silence, complete silence.

Mr. Rogers takes stock of the room. He realizes the children are, in their way, testing him. He pauses.

What Fred Rogers was to offer was nothing short of a masterclass in how to use emotional intelligence.

If we understand emotional intelligence to be only about introspection and empathy and not about we and environment, then we are only looking at one piece of the puzzle.

If Mr. Rogers had focused only on empathy, he may have said something like, "It's a shame that happened. I'm sorry." Or maybe he would have said that we have to be careful with toys.

Instead, he did something different.

Why Leaders Wear Sweaters - How to Practice Empathy

As he paused, Mr. Rogers considered the context of his environment. **He considered the *we* in the room, not just the *me*. He considered not just himself or even just the boy as an individual, but the whole class of children.** He put himself in the shoes of the child and realized that there were two important matters—the stuffed animal itself, and the question of whether *his* ear could be ripped off too.

First, Mr. Rogers did in fact tell the child he was sorry about his stuffed animal—in other words, **he expressed empathy. And then he did something more, he drilled down to the root cause of the boy's comment and said something to address and change the environment.** He assured the children they needn't fear when something like that happens.

"Sometimes that happens to toys, doesn't it? Their ears come off or their legs come off," he said. "But that never happens to us. Our ears don't come off, our noses don't come off. Our arms don't come off."

"And our legs don't come off!" the boy exclaimed.

Immediately, all of the other children started asking questions, and *poignant* questions.

Mr. Rogers had passed the test. He was still in touch with childhood, in touch with the fears that needed to be assuaged in order to build trust.

Get Over Yourself - The Biggest Mistake People Make with EQ

When I ask people what they think of when they hear the phrase "emotional intelligence," all too often it's centered on *me*. They say things like, "know your own personal competencies" and "be self-aware." They say EQ is "managing my emotions." And I can't blame them.

Most of the literature out there focuses on how managers can increase their EQ for their own benefit.[11] The articles often follow a similar pattern: do some soulsearching to understand yourself better, build and express empathy, then benefit by earning the trust of your employees or gaining a promotion. The problem is, just **focusing on yourself as an isolated individual who simply responds to others' provocations leaves out a crucial element.**

Your emotional intelligence isn't just about recognizing and exercising your own emotional life and strengths: it's also about perceiving and connecting with your environment and the emotional lives of those around you.

In the case of Mr. Rogers, he not only made the children feel good, but also earned the trust of the room because his answer showed them he not only cared about them, but that he *understood* them. He acknowledged the boy and *then he changed the dynamic of the room* by addressing the group's unstated fear.

It was a win-win. Mr. Rogers gained their trust and the children gained a sense of security.

WHAT DOES EMPATHY LOOK LIKE?

Observing what others say & do

Inferring & drawing out what others think & feel

Genuine understanding

1.3 ## What Is Holistic Emotional Intelligence?

OK—you may be thinking, Puppets? Children? How seriously can we take this? Yet Fred Rogers was successful in his work because his assumption was both simple and radical; he believed that children had deep emotions, just like adults. He understood people's need to feel safe and accepted, and to understand what is happening around us. On the surface, the children's emotional distress seemed to be centered around a stuffed animal, but at its core, the distress was about something much deeper: can my head come off too?

And that desire to belong, be accepted, and feel safe extends to adults as well. Core desires drive our feelings and our behavior individually and collectively. Your colleagues and employees (likely) aren't children, and you're (likely) not putting on a puppet show, but the skills needed to perceive your environment are the same.

Working to understand our own motivations, the motivations of others, and the way our environment impacts these motivations is what holistic emotional intelligence is about.

When we can understand these motivators, it's good for *me and* it's good for *we.*

Collaboration is hard. It takes EQ to do it effectively.

On our own, we tend to be more selfish and will often not collaborate well.[12] It's hard because we often have to do something most of us aren't very good at: perspective taking. Perspective taking involves a thought process (cognitive) that is different than empathy. Empathy is feeling another person's feelings while perspective taking is taking someone else's viewpoint into account. It becomes even harder if it's a team where everyone is out for themselves. You have to overcome the temptation to be selfish and that takes discipline.

But if you do, it pays off. Teams that collaborate effectively outperform other teams that might have a smarter person or a higher average intellect.[13] They're amazing at innovating and solving problems, which boosts their collective intelligence. Why? They're communicating well and allowing all perspectives to be considered. They get into the shoes of the other person to understand. They determine how to support each other. This creates the environment that encourages brainstorming and unique approaches to solving problems. When you design an environment that leads to greater collaboration, people are willing to engage above and beyond what's required to make the group succeed. And so they're more collectively intelligent.

When we understand EQ as a skill that requires an appraisal of environmental factors, we begin to grasp the potential of emotional intelligence. *Part of your responsibility as a leader is to recognize the why, understand others' needs, and adjust your environment to create a positive impact.*

Holistic emotional intelligence is about understanding *why* something matters—what's at stake for the individual employee—*and how* the environment shapes decision-making.

1.4 Case Study: When *We* Works for Everyone

Recently, I was called in to work with an engineering plant to help them improve their team and systems. The products this company makes have very little room for error, and the stakes are high. If the team isn't accurate, then errors can cause a lot of harm.

The company was having problems with a manager, whom I'll call "Alex." Alex was a people-pleaser. He was a nice guy who connected his self-worth to whether or not people liked him. When people wanted critical feedback to improve their work and reduce their errors, they went around Alex and asked his boss or other employees for help. They knew that going to Alex would mean only praise, whether or not it was warranted. He failed to give constructive feedback, which inevitably resulted in problems.

Alex had, in effect, lost credibility and trust with his team, so everything around him had started to unravel. At first it was slow, but like water swirling around a drain, it started to move more and more quickly.

Now, if we were to apply only the popular version of emotional intelligence here, what would we tell Alex to do?

We might say Alex needed to take a hard look at himself. Once he did, he would realize that he was people-pleasing because of a need to be liked, and that need was harmful to the work culture and the company. We'd remind him that it's impossible to please everyone, and that trying to do so was harming his work and relationships with others.

And that might even work. For a short time.

But here's the problem: it would be temporary. In fact, the team leaders had already tried telling Alex to change. It failed for a predictable reason.

Telling someone to change without helping them to change their environment rarely leads to success.

Here's another way to look at it: If you wanted to quit eating junk food, would you continue to buy chips and candy and keep them around your house? Or would you change your environment whenever you could? If you wanted to quit smoking, wouldn't you start by throwing out your cigarettes?

What wasn't being considered was the *why* behind his people-pleasing. They didn't have a system in place to show Alex the impact and cost of covering for his employees.

Alex needed to change, but he needed his environment to support that change.

That's the often overlooked element of exercising emotional intelligence—looking as deeply at the environment we are operating in as we do at ourselves.

Just telling Alex to better know his own tendencies *without* changing the environmental factors that triggered those tendencies is a Band-Aid when you need a suture.

1.5 The Three Elements of Change

By the time I was asked to work with the executives at Alex's company, they were facing high rates of turnover. The data I collected showed a lack of engagement across the board. In one instance, another executive voiced her lack of trust in Alex because he had attempted to protect an employee by covering up their error-ridden work. Alex had claimed, "We can't expect this person to be perfect." It left the other executives wondering if they could trust Alex at all. They felt they needed a management team that consistently held people accountable.

So, what did we do?

The company had invested a lot of time, energy, and resources in Alex. They didn't want to see him go; they just wanted to see him change. So we focused on three things:

Element 1 **SELF RECOGNITION**

We spent time doing one-on-one individual work so that he could begin to recognize when he was engaging in counterproductive behavior. Was he doing what was needed or just telling people what they wanted to hear?

Element 2 **SOCIAL RECOGNITION**

Alex's assignment was to begin to observe and investigate how his people-pleasing was impacting his team. After asking for feedback from one of the supervisors that reported to him, he was surprised and disappointed by what he heard. The supervisor recounted a recent situation when Alex reversed a tough decision to send an employee home after a safety incident. The supervisor told Alex how this had undermined him.

Alex finally began to see the impact. He had never seen it because he had never asked; doing so caused him to take a hard look at the consequences.

Element 3 **DESIGN STRUCTURE**

Finally, I worked with Alex and his colleagues to create structure within his environment for addressing his people-pleasing tendencies. We designed a system for tracking accountability. Alex liked metrics. He began to track when an issue first surfaced, the number of days until it was resolved, the resolution, and the impact to the team. The final piece was getting feedback from his team to determine if they felt the issues were resolved. Alex began to see the value in feedback and recognized that it was key to keeping him from avoiding issues. Avoiding the hard stuff was his emotional reaction.

It was a reaction based in fear. Once he was finally resolving issues, his team and the CEO recognized his efforts. Suddenly positive reinforcements began coming in from all over—other executives, me, his team members.

And what happened?

Alex started to rely less on his need for people to like him. He was able to be more objective with his decision-making because we set up an environment where objective decisions were rewarded.

We had identified the problem, the impact it was having, and then created environmental checkpoints that would support the change Alex was trying to make.

Teamwork and collaboration improved in his department because Alex was no longer inhibiting his team's ability to learn from mistakes. When Alex finally realized what was at stake, he realized that his own need for approval was getting in the way of what his team truly needed.

These weren't earth-shattering changes. They were relatively small habits that made a big difference. His department's employee engagement started rising.

What Alex's intervention and the Mr. Rogers story have in common is this: in both instances, the application of emotional intelligence is about more than just *me* or the individual or the self. It was about their role within their environment—for Mr. Rogers, it was a trusted adult and for Alex it was an effective manager. It's easy to think about EQ as being all empathy, all compassion, all *feeling*. But it's also about *design*. How can you address the classroom in such a way that it eases all of the children's fears? How can you create an environment that enables people to work with their strengths, weaknesses, and quirks to do their jobs well?

Smart leaders engineer their environments to support emotionally intelligent decisions.

Our emotional intelligence exists within an ecosystem, a community. The brain's reactions are essential and they're hardwired into us, whether it's the classroom or the boardroom. And in order to achieve growth— whether in ourselves or someone else—we need to understand the people and their individual motivators and perspectives, as well as the way that environment is affecting us.

How to Put the Three Elements of Change to Work

Take a moment, write down your thoughts about...

→ **Self Recognition:**
What is one behavior you'd like to change that would make a positive impact and contribute to your success?

→ **Social Recognition:**
What has been the negative impact of this behavior on others? If you don't know, ask for feedback.

→ **Design Structure:**
What do you need to change in your environment that would help you make that behavioral change? What hinders or helps your progress?

**CHAPTER SUMMARY:
THREE THINGS TO REMEMBER**

→ Most people think EQ is just about *me*, but really it's *we*. Emotional intelligence isn't just about recognizing and exercising your own emotional life and strengths; it's also about perceiving and connecting with your environment and the emotional lives of those around you.

→ Working to understand our own motivations, the motivations of others, and the way our environment impacts these motivations is what holistic emotional intelligence is about.

→ Holistic emotional intelligence is also about understanding why something matters—what's at stake for the individual employee—and how the workplace environment shapes decision-making, innovation, and relationships.

CHAPTER 2

Fear, Threats, And The Way Our Brains Perceive Our Environments

Pick a hand.

Now look down at your hand. Fold the thumb in toward the palm and bend the other fingers down to make a fist. This fist is a crude representation of your brain. If you want to begin to understand the emotional part of emotional intelligence, then start with your hand.

Your wrist would be the brainstem, the oldest part of the brain in terms of human development. It's connected to your breath, your heartbeat, and other essentials. The thumb represents the limbic system. The limbic system is responsible for our emotions and is deep in the brain.

The four folded fingers are a rough rendering of the prefrontal cortex, which is the rational part of the brain that most of us would *like* to think drives our thoughts and actions it's the part of the brain that's in charge of analysis, problem-solving, and reasoning. And it's what Nobel Prize winner Daniel Kahneman calls System 2, where we are "thinking slow."[14] It's also a part of the brain that takes *a lot of energy* to do its job. We need energy in the prefrontal cortex for creative, strategic thinking. The prefrontal cortex has the power to think about thinking. But the power of the prefrontal cortex is also its problem—this part of the brain wants to use energy while the rest of the body is programmed to conserve energy.

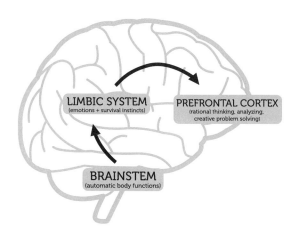

Fifty thousand.

That's the estimated average number of thoughts the brain has each day.[15] That's a lot of work for one organ to do. The brain comprises only 3% of our body mass, yet it consumes more than 20% of our energy.[16] This is why the instinct of the brain is to rely less on the prefrontal cortex—that high-energy consumer—and more on the autopilot of the limbic system.

For example, answer this:

What's 1+1?

Easy. You probably think I'm joking.

What's 2+2?

Same thing. You might be wondering, what's the catch?

What's 257+79?

Now, before you start to puzzle it out, what was your immediate reaction? My guess is that you felt a little bit uncomfortable and you might not have wanted to crunch the numbers. Perhaps you even reached for your phone or started to carry the one. This discomfort is your brain moving past autopilot and into reasoning.

Here's another way of thinking of it: Let's say I asked you to think about what a dog looks like. Go ahead and picture it. I bet it came to mind quickly.

What about a cat? How does that look? You likely called up an image instantaneously.

Now, what will your life look like in ten years?

That question is far harder. It requires the prefrontal cortex to answer, and we resist it.[17]

Whether or not we want to admit it, neuroscience research shows that most decision-making starts in our limbic system. In other words, our emotions (and not our logic) help us make decisions.

It's the impressions and feelings formed by our limbic system that guide our decisions. Then, we use the prefrontal cortex (our four folded fingers) to justify decisions that align with these instinctive impressions.[18]

We think we're making decisions logically, but it's just the opposite. We make decisions using our limbic system or our "gut" and then we rationalize it. The limbic system is more prone to errors and is more impulsive. And contrary to popular belief, our gut is not right most of the time.[19]

This can feel unsettling at first, because many of us want to believe we're rational creatures who come to our conclusions thoughtfully and after conscious deliberation. But the truth is, the brain has a lot of inputs to process every single day, and when given the chance, it will revert to autopilot.

2.1 Don't Fight Your Brain, Embrace It

To understand holistic emotional intelligence, which sees the individual as part of and influenced by environment, you must know the following:

The brain is old, and it takes time to adjust.

The outside world moves very quickly. As a species, we don't have as many physical threats now as we used to, but we do have social threats.

A cohesive emotional intelligence understands that even though we're living in the twenty-first century, we're still operating with brains that are very, very old.

The most emotionally intelligent people understand that being on the lookout for threats is a natural and essential part of how the brain perceives the world, whether it's the threat of a lion making a move on your tribe or the threat of losing your job.

The good news?

We can use emotional intelligence to navigate these perceived threats.

Here's how. First and foremost, **stop trying to fight the brain and instead work with it.** Our behaviors are driven by the pursuit of safety and the need to connect with others. We need to understand and accept this fact, otherwise we will operate on autopilot, all the while not realizing that the unconscious brain is driving us and others. And if we don't know what emotions are in the driver's seat, we might not like our destination.

Do you remember Alex, the people-pleasing manager from Chapter 1? His need to be liked was causing his whole team to derail. He was forgoing opportunities to give important critical feedback and simply became the friendly boss that gave people whatever they wanted.

Alex's need to be liked was coming from his limbic system—the deep brain. He was worried that saying no to his colleagues or giving them difficult feedback would dissolve his relationships with them, which would feel a lot like a threat to his safety and stability at the company.

Fear of rejection causes us to feel unsafe and that causes a chemical reaction in our brain.

We often think of the word "safe" in terms of physical safety, but neuroscientists have discovered that people seek safety on many different levels—and the brain registers those kinds of safety (social, physical) in the same way. Neuroscientist Evian Gordon says the fundamental organizing principle of the brain is to minimize danger and maximize reward.[20]

Think back to our ancestors and their survival. What helped our ancestors survive in harsh conditions? What would have happened if they'd wandered off in the forest by themselves? The protection, collaboration, and resources that being in a group implied ensured safety. Through forming groups or tribes, our chances of survival increase considerably. Our brains know this. They've been hardwired to recognize this. The brain is a social organ. In fact, research from Dr. James Coan tells us our brains won't fully thrive unless part of a group.[21]

Forming a group doesn't just imply physical safety. It implies belonging.

Neuroscientists have also shown that social pain registers the same as physical pain.[22] **The brain is constantly scanning for social threats to status or challenges to your role in your particular group.**[23]

I feel pain if I fall on the ice and break my arm, and I also feel pain if my boss berates me at work in front of my peers. Social pain, we have come to learn, registers in the brain in the same way as physical pain. In fact, there was a study conducted that indicated just like you can take an ibuprofen to ease physical pain, you can also take an ibuprofen to reduce social pain.[24] The brain identifies social needs with survival.

When we do identify a social pain, which part of the brain responds? You guessed it—the limbic system. We respond with very little thought, *because* the brain has identified social pain as a threat to survival, just like physical pain.

We can blame our ancestors, or we can learn to work with them.

2.2 The "Fight-or-Flight" Response

Most of us have heard the term *fight-or-flight*. We think of this, usually, as being a reaction to a physical threat. Someone is attacking or coming at us: do we run like hell or do we kick and punch our way out?

SOARING BEYOND FIGHT-OR-FLIGHT

Dr. David Rock, Director of the NeuroLeadership Institute, coined the acronym SCARF to highlight the five social domains your limbic brain is always scanning to keep you safe: status, certainty, autonomy, relatedness, and fairness.

To learn more about using the SCARF Model to create a trigger-free environment for your employees, visit:www.thinkaperio.com/eq3book.

But what we don't always recognize is that fight-or-flight is not just a reaction to physical danger, and occurs just as often in contexts that threaten our sense of emotional stability.

The difficulty is that emotional fight-or-flight is more subtle, and harder to recognize.

I recently worked with one of the younger managers at a client's corporate office who I'll call "Jasper." "The CEO is trying to get rid of me," Jasper confided. He was just sure he was going to be fired.

"Why do you think that?" I asked.

He said he wasn't sure, exactly, but he knew they were talking about firing him. When I pressed him further, he said he knew the CEO had a meeting with the COO and that they were talking about him.

"Really?" I asked, "How do you know that?"
"I can just tell," Jasper said.

My advice was for Jasper to talk to the CEO to avoid stewing over it. He didn't, and instead let a week go by.

What do you think happened to his productivity that week? It was terrible. He continued to scan his environment, looking for reasons to back up his hypothesis that he was going to be fired. He couldn't focus, so his work suffered. It was a self-fulfilling prophecy.

In other words, he was in flight mode, fleeing the problem and fleeing his work.

Soon enough, Jasper found out the truth. It turns out, the CEO *was* talking about him—Jasper's instincts were right. But his assumptions were wrong. The CEO was working with the COO to plan a party celebrating Jasper's upcoming wedding.

When a threat response is triggered, we are more prone to draw incorrect conclusions and become much less productive. The stress associated with the perceived threat diminishes our ability to do energy-intensive work in the brain like creativity, problem-solving skills, our ability to draw insight, and our analytic thinking skills.[25]

With a threat, the prefrontal cortex shuts down so the limbic brain can scan for threats and look for confirmation. Had Jasper noticed that he was responding with a flight mode and gone to talk to the CEO about his hunch, his week would have been radically different.

Emotional intelligence requires that we recognize when we are perceiving a threat and then resist the impulse to go into fight-or-flight mode.

The more you practice reading your responses to your environment, the more effective you'll be at making more objective and intentional decisions, and the more confident and productive you will be at the workplace.

This also requires that leaders create environments that do not trigger employees by:

→ Clearly communicating expectations;

→ Recognizing jobs well done;

→ Creating autonomy by letting them make decisions and have control where appropriate;

→ Creating a sense of team identity to foster collaboration;[26] and

→ Treating employees fairly.[27]

As a leader, every decision you make either triggers a social threat in your team, or creates a sense of safety, reinforcing higher-level thinking through allowing the prefrontal cortex to shine. That's why leadership is so hard. Smart leaders often trigger threat responses unintentionally, and are then left scratching their heads as to why they didn't get the results they wanted. Emotionally intelligent leaders understand the threat response and its effects and adapt their behavior accordingly.

> *"Good leaders need to be skilled entrepreneurs of identity."*
>
> *- Alex Haslam[28]*

2.3 The Sad Rise of Blame-Shifting

The most *common* version of "fight" I see in the corporate world is blame-shifting.

It's not my fault, it's someone else's, is almost always the subtext or outright message of someone in fight-or-flight mode.

Take, for example, Rachel, a manager I work with at a pharmaceutical company. She was called out by her manager for not hitting her goals. She immediately felt the social threat.

VISIT ONLINE RESOURCES FOR:

A quick assessment to spot your most dominant triggers.

Her response: "It's not our fault. We're being given faulty data from another department and we get blamed for it. We're last in line, so we get stuck holding the bag."

But her blame-shifting to another department did not fix the problem. In the moment, if Rachel had realized that she was responding with her "fight" impulse, she could have paused.

She could have labeled what she was feeling as a way to minimize its power over her, "This is fight" or "This is me feeling threatened."

If she had done that, she would have been exercising emotional intelligence on an individual level. In this case, Rachel could have paused, labeled her "fight," and realized her manager wanted to get to the root of the problem, solve it, and hit the company's goals. To accomplish this, she didn't need to blame. She needed to be curious and get to the root issue.

Blaming others often feeds the limbic brain's fear and blocks emotional intelligence.

The pause would have given her some distance to see herself responding to her environment, notice it, and then adjust her response to address both herself and her environment. If you are unable to do this in the moment, it's not too late. Take time later to reflect on the situation and your response and decide the best course of action.

Labeling our emotions (e.g., "fear," "anger," "disappointment"), even in the most basic way, creates distance between ourselves and our emotions because it requires observation of ourselves. When we apply a label, the limbic brain can reduce the level of the threat and lower the reactive response.[29] The problem shifts from being felt by the limbic system to being analyzed by the prefrontal cortex.

2.4 Why We Tend to Focus on the Negative

Neuroscientists say the limbic brain, which controls emotions, is like a squirrel: hyper attentive but not very smart.[30]

It's not very smart, they say, because it will often assume the negative. On some level we know this—it's why we hear people lament how someone else "always assumes the worst." What about our environments leads us to assume the worst?

Again, think about our ancestors. Let's say they encountered a threat, like a lion. Would it have done them any good to sit around analyzing the lion? They didn't ask, "How many feet away do you think that lion is? What speed do you think we should run?" Of course not. They simply saw a threat and reacted as quickly as they could. In the case of threat, their cortisol levels rose, adrenaline spiked, heart rate and breath quickened, and pupils might even dilate.

This instinct to react quickly to a perceived threat instead of pausing to analyze whether it really is a threat, is the same impulse that makes humans so willing to believe the negative over the positive.

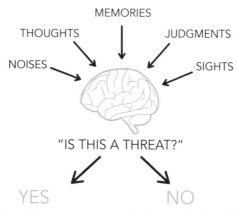

The brain is wired to evaluate every situation as a
"THREAT" or "NOT A THREAT"

MEMORIES

THOUGHTS   JUDGMENTS

NOISES   SIGHTS

"IS THIS A THREAT?"

YES   NO

- Brain decides between fight, flight, & freeze
- Coritsol & adrenaline produced
- Pupils dialate, heart rate increases, breathing quickens
- Contributes to experiencing stress & anxiety

- Brain senses "safety" allowing energy to go toward analytical thinking & creativity
- Your body is able to rest & digest
- Contributes to experiencing a sense of peace & calm

Threats have a deeper and longer impact than rewards because the brain wants to keep us alive, and taking risks in the face of potential danger is not worth it.[31] In other words, better safe than sorry. Studies even show that employees perform best, and even marriages thrive the most, when individuals receive praise and criticism at a five-to-one ratio.[32]

It takes five positives to counteract one negative in the brain.

When I facilitate emotional intelligence trainings, I too fall into this trap of letting the negative outweigh the positive. The room might be 97% engaged and I might receive overwhelmingly positive feedback, but I tend to focus automatically on the person on their cell phone who seems bored. I have to remind myself not to fixate on them, and this takes brain discipline. It helps to label it, "Ahh, there goes my limbic brain, activated by a social threat."[33]

When the limbic brain is triggered, it hijacks the thinking side of our brain. With the slightest trigger, our ability to apply reason and logic can drop by

75 percent.

It's worth repeating, the brain is old, and it takes time to adjust.

Being emotionally intelligent means keeping in mind how the human brain naturally functions. And then working with it.

This means giving yourself pause to notice how you're responding. It means realizing that we tend to assume the worst, and working against that habit. And it means building environments that keep in mind these ancient patterns of the brain so that employees can be empowered to do their best work.

2.5   How to Evaluate Your Decision-Making

→ Know thyself. Practice self-awareness. Imagine you are someone else and objectively observe your own behavior. What do you see?

→ Consider previous stressful situations that triggered the fight-or-flight response. When did you get blamed for someone else's failures, criticized unfairly, or realize you were unprepared? Did you feel your heart rate increase, your face heating up, your mouth going dry, knots in your stomach? How did you respond? Did you engage in a heated debate, blame others or the situation, or feel like you wanted to run from the room?

→ How did the fight-or-flight response impact you? Did you feel out of control, like a victim, or were you embarrassed?

→ What patterns do you notice about your triggers?

→ How would you respond differently if you could do it over again?

→ How do you balance strong emotional experiences? Do you read, do yoga, play sports, meditate, or pray?

→ When do you fall prey to fundamental attribution error, our tendency to judge others, and make assumptions that result in blame? The next time you get triggered, try assuming positive intent.

**DOWNLOAD:
DECISION-MAKING TOOLS**

Resources designed to help you and your team improve your decision-making are available at thinkaperio.com/eq3book

**CHAPTER SUMMARY:
THREE THINGS TO REMEMBER**

→ The latest research shows that we make most of our decisions starting in our limbic system, or primitive emotional center. Emotional intelligence requires that we recognize when we are perceiving a threat and then resist the impulse to go into fight-or-flight mode.

→ What most people don't recognize is that fight-or-flight is not just a reaction to physical danger, this response also occurs when our sense of social and emotional safety is threatened. Leaders often unintentionally trigger threat responses in the workplace and are left scratching their heads as to why they didn't get the results they wanted.

→ Emotionally intelligent leaders work to adapt their behavior and office environments to minimize employees' threat responses and maximize their safety, productivity, and creativity. High EQ leaders are more likely to make better decisions, influence more effectively, and design the right environment to succeed.

CHAPTER 3

How Courage Drives Emotional Intelligence

In *The Wizard of Oz*, when Dorothy and her friends set off on that yellow brick road, they needed three things to succeed: a heart, a brain, and courage.[34]

Most of the time, when people think of emotional intelligence, they think only of heart. They think heart = empathy, compassion, and kindness.

But, as we saw in Chapter 1, *emotionally intelligent* people who are full of heart—like Fred Rogers—possess more than just feelings of empathy. They *act* as leaders by considering the needs of others and working to shape their environment to help others to thrive.

Then, of course, there's the brain. If the scarecrow "only had a brain," he would have had to respond to the same hardwiring of the limbic system that we humans have to contend with. This is a lesser-known aspect of emotional intelligence, but it's crucial. As we saw in Chapter 2, understanding how the brain works and how it has evolved over time is essential to understanding our own reactions, the reactions of others, and how we create environments that move people to be creative and innovative.

So what of the lion and the final element?

That's where you come in as a leader. **Emotional intelligence requires courage.** It takes guts to move beyond yourself and try to shape your office's current environment. **Leaders fail to adapt when they fail to bring together all the pieces: heart, brain, and courage.**

True emotional intelligence takes heart (empathy and compassion), an understanding of the brain (its fears and tendencies), and courage to change the environment to bring these components together.

3.1 How to Create a Better Environment

How do we bring all these pieces together? How do we create this environment?

When I begin work with a client, my first step is to try to understand the relevant environment as best I can. This helps pave the way for conversations about tough topics and requires a particular mindset.

First, I don't assume anything. I enter the situation with an open mind. Questions are at the center of my approach.

Second, I enter without judgment. When I say "judgment," I don't mean just deciding if something is good or bad, I mean I *try to hold off on making conclusions.*

The brain always wants to find patterns and make connections, so it takes a lot of mental energy to put aside assumptions and try to see what really is.

It takes courage to challenge and put aside my assumptions because it means I have to admit that I don't know the answer. I don't know what I'll find when I enter without judgment, and I have to be willing to find anything. For leaders, this means there's a possibility of seeing your own mistakes reflected back at you.

Third, my aim is to build trust and listen. My goal in the listening phase is to turn that sense-making instinct down for a little while and try to collect as much information and input as I can.

Listen first, analyze later.

In turn, people find themselves able to confide in me. This process allows me to not only see the environment for what it is, but to start to uncover the many factors that go into making things the way they are.

THE PATH TOWARD TRUST: OPEN-MINDED MANAGEMENT

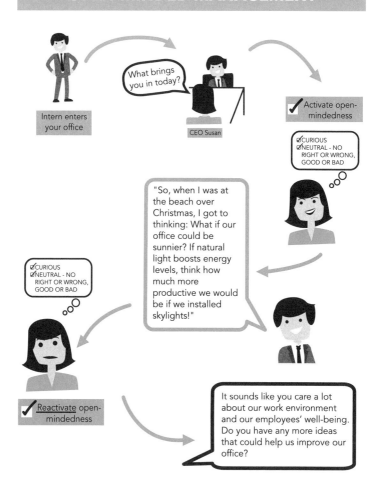

3.2 Getting to the Root: How to Ask Courageous Questions

Some of the questions I ask when I'm in this diagnostic phase include:

→ What is the problem? Why do we want to solve it?

→ What is causing your problems or what is not happening or not functioning?

→ What is the opportunity in this issue?

→ If our problems could be resolved, what would change?

→ What's the gap between where we want to be and our current state?

→ What are the key drivers that would close that gap?

→ If there is a conflict with someone else, what do you agree on?

→ What are the points of disagreement?

→ What has to be done to get over the points of disagreement?

→ What impact is the problem having on your ability to be successful? Why?

→ Try to consolidate the problem down to a decision.

→ Is there more detail you can gather about the problem? Explain.

→ Is the problem something you can resolve on your own?

→ Do multiple people need to be involved?

→ Where are you most likely to fail at something that is also critical to solving the problem?

→ Would it help to find a way to collaborate differently?

These questions might seem relatively simple, but when you have the courage to ask them and keep an open mind, they often yield significant answers.

This open-mindedness takes courage because it means you are willing to fully hear the responses from people without dismissing their concerns or becoming defensive.

3.3 Start With Clearly Identifying the Threats

As a leader, this can be tough. You might find critiques of your previous decisions or your leadership style. But if you want to build a truly emotionally intelligent environment that positions employees to excel, you need to practice the kind of listening where you can take ideas and concerns seriously without feeling the need to explain or defend yourself.

After listening to the answers to these questions, I begin to diagnose the problem. Often, it has to do with threats. **Threat trumps reward so identifying and removing threats are the first order of business.**

Common threats are: [35]

- Lack of clarity
- Competing priorities
- Lack of autonomy
- The fear of failure
- Lack of recognition and validation
- Lack of fairness

It's only through listening without judgment or defense–which requires high emotional intelligence–that I can get to the root of the problem.

Case Study: Why No Man Is An Island (Not Even You, Patrick)

3.4

Take Patrick, a CEO I worked with. After my process of gathering feedback from his employees in their environment and diagnosing the problem, a common thread eventually emerged: Patrick wasn't including the right people in his decision-making.

If he was going to fix this and become a better leader, he needed to improve his emotional intelligence and his interpersonal skills. He also needed to quit his habit of micromanaging his employees.

Employees would tell me about his (micro)managing style during my one-on-one interviews. Several were at the end of their ropes "If he wants to do my job," they'd say, "then let him have it!"

Patrick was activating a threat response in his employees by challenging their autonomy.

So, what did most of the employees do?

Let's remember the limbic brain–the emotional center of the brain–from Chapter 2. Four high-ranking colleagues at this company responded with "flight." They checked out, either mentally or physically, by relinquishing their remaining autonomy. They piled any mistakes, challenges, or problems onto Patrick's back instead of taking responsibility because they figured it didn't matter. He would just do what he wanted to do anyway.

Three of his colleagues responded with "fight." They got higher-ups involved and worked to get the CEO fired rather than addressing their concerns directly with Patrick. Patrick realized he was in trouble, so he started to involve others. He tried to back off on some of the micromanaging and let his employees do their work. He even realized he needed to ask for feedback, so he brought them into the decision-making process and validated them by telling them he appreciated their feedback and input.

But in private, he still wasn't doing the work to become more emotionally intelligent.

Though Patrick had begun to make a change, he hadn't done so for the right reasons, or under the right influences. He was responding to poor employee engagement and trouble from the top, and his efforts were insincere. **He thought he could suppress his urge to micromanage by appearing to change, but no genuine change had occurred.**

For instance, even though he was seeking the counsel of other employees, he usually did so after he had already made a decision. It didn't take long for his team to catch on. The other leaders quickly realized what was happening and it made things worse. Patrick wasn't just a micromanager, he was now a "manipulator" in the eyes of his employees. His colleagues had been tricked into thinking he wanted their input when he never really did. Trust was all but eroded.

But why did Patrick feel the need to micromanage? It would have helped to ask this long before things got to this point, but there we were.

Remember the limbic brain, or the emotional center? Patrick's limbic brain was being activated by a threat. He didn't think his team was going to be able to hit their big goal. He needed this goal. His legacy was at stake.

When leaders are uncertain and don't feel like they have control, the limbic brain responds: *I need more control. I will only be certain if I dictate every detail.*

So, Patrick and I worked together to address the underlying threat to his response. I asked Patrick what he was most afraid of and then began to explore more deeply.

He was afraid of not hitting his goal.

OK. Why?

"Well, I don't know if I have the right team in place."

"What team members do you feel are misplaced or missing altogether?" I asked.

"Well, we need another data person and well…now that I think about it, I guess the crux of the problem is that I don't think they are bringing the right people into the meetings. I worry they're making decisions without bringing in the data analysts and marketing group. I'm worried they're not cross-collaborating effectively. The executives seem to want to only meet with executives, but to get the right people in the room who know the data and can move the initiatives forward, we have to go across titles."

Patrick had an uncertainty problem on his hands and needed to find a better way to communicate. If the right people weren't invited to the table, and if the environment wasn't set up to allow the needed cross-collaboration, it's no wonder his instinct was to try to clamp down and manage it all.

Emotionally intelligent leaders understand what's at stake if they give in to the impulse to over-control. They'll trigger the threat response in their teams.

In order to authentically build trust, Patrick needed to identify what was at stake (why), determine the needs of his team, and help his team change the environment accordingly.

The case of Patrick is not unique. Leaders are not immune to threats. His management caused his team to move into *fight-or-flight* mode—the result of the limbic brain kicking into gear. Then he responded— but his response was an emotional response triggered by a threat. We all know people who have done something like this. Patrick simply tried to muster up the *appearance* of change in order to cope with his own fear of being fired. He needed the emotional intelligence to rise above fight-or-flight mode and into analysis so he could eliminate both the threats he and his employees were sensing. He needed to understand himself and his environment in order to instigate real change. And that shift—from understanding an individual's needs to working to shape their environment to meet those needs—takes courage.

3.5 How to Use Pauses to Strategically Overcome Fear

It takes courage to both seek out the root of a problem and to identify it. Feedback can come externally, like the interviews with employees at Patrick's company, but it can also come internally. If we practice the emotional intelligence to recognize our own fear-based reactions, we can practice responding to our emotions as they arise in an emotionally intelligent way.

When I was first asked to write a curriculum for a personal development course at a graduate school, I hesitated. I thought about it for a few days. Then I decided I needed to be pushed beyond my comfort zone and this was a great opportunity to reach students.

I said yes.

Then I panicked.

The graduate school program began to move forward with questions you might expect: How many credit hours should the course be? How should we test students on the curriculum?

I froze. "What in the world did I get myself into?" I wondered. My brain moved to high alert. I felt a threat. My credibility and my ideas were on the line. I pulled away from others and hunkered down, mired in worry. I fretted.

After a little while, I was able to realize what I was doing. It was my limbic brain jumping into action again, trying to come to the rescue. Its sole function, as we know, is to keep us alive. And we know that keeping us alive includes social elements. Humans are hardwired to be social because once upon a time we needed groups to survive. Inclusion was essential.

Taking on this new challenge sparked fear: fear I would fail and lose the respect of my peers or, at worst, lose altogether the community I counted on. The fear wasn't rational, but it was deep-seated and it was driving my actions.

So, what did I do?

Well, first I froze.

Freezing is different from "the pause" I encourage in earlier chapters, because freezing is about locking up in fear.

Taking a pause means you recognize the fear, take a beat, and step away from it to consider how it's influencing you and your perception of your environment. Freezing, on the other hand, is being paralyzed by fear, and letting your limbic brain dictate how you respond.

Even though I had the emotional intelligence to realize that what I was feeling was pure, limbic-brain-driven fear, I still let it drive my behavior.

I waited to do what I knew to do: tackle it. I'm telling you this because it's normal to recognize the emotion and still feel so attached to it that you can't separate yourself enough to act. But as you might guess, problems arise when we wait too long.

WHY IT PAYS TO DISCUSS PROBLEMS IMMEDIATELY

The health of a team, as discussed in *Harvard Business Review,* is measured by the "average lag time between identifying and discussing problems." When there is a shorter lag time, problems are solved faster and the resolution betters relationships. With a longer lag time, "the more room for mistrust, dysfunction, and more tangible costs." Courage is good for people and it's good for outcomes.

After weeks of not asking for help, I realized I had two choices: (1) Ask for help from my community of people in my field, or (2) Fail miserably. I was certain that, with choice #1, I'd look like an idiot. Still, I decided, I'd rather try than let the program down. I swallowed my pride, which is another way of saying I let myself be vulnerable. I asked for help.

Later that day, I checked my inbox. I couldn't believe how quickly the colleagues in my community had responded to my requests for help. A mentor and friend who had curricula at several other universities had written back immediately.

"No problem," he said. "I'm going to send you my structure that you can use as a guide."

I exhaled a huge breath that I didn't know I was holding. I felt energy and confidence reenter my body. I knew that, with support, I could turn my work into a curriculum and meet the program's needs and guidelines. I couldn't believe how much easier it had become after I realized I had help and guidance.

But then again, I could. What do we know about the brain? According to social neuroscientists, our brains are designed to connect and interact with others, especially during times of stress. We are hardwired to be in a group because we survived for a long time by sticking to our tribe. A significant part of the brain is devoted to acquiring safe and secure connections that help us face challenges and danger. Alone and isolated, my task felt impossible. But once I brought in others—and not just any group but a group I trusted—I was able to turn off the emotional part of my brain and activate the thinking part. Creative problem-solving was possible again.

Employing emotional intelligence helps us to see patterns of the brain, and then allows for the courage to address them.

In this case, that meant reaching out to my community for support.

3.6 Integrating the Elements of EQ

The courage of emotional intelligence lies in recognizing the limbic brain's response, identifying what's at stake, and then making a choice about how to respond. It's about making the unconscious conscious. Without this ability to read and respond to yourself, fear and habit will keep you on autopilot. If I had reached out earlier for my curriculum project, I would have spent less time worrying and more time working with my community to find a solution. Change gives us a chance to see who our community is and how they support us.

WHY FREAKING OUT IS GOOD (SOMETIMES)

The limbic system is so deeply wired to keep us alive that it freaks out at the slightest hint of every potential threat. This is the default mode. It is our habitual pattern. We even have special words for those who ignore the warnings. If they ignore the warnings and fail, we call them foolish. If they ignore the warnings and succeed, we call them courageous. At our core, we are all cowardly lions.

Integrating emotional intelligence requires that you recognize when your limbic brain is riding roughshod over reason.

It can feel good, in the moment, to make the decision without stakeholders or work from a place of worry, but you will pay in one way or another.

Do you want to be intentional with a lasting, positive long-term solution, or take a short cut and sacrifice what's at stake? Take, for example, one of the biggest destroyers of problem solving: conflict avoidance. We avoid addressing issues and rationalize our behavior by saying it will work itself out. "It will go away," we think, and we hope for the best. "The best" rarely happens. It usually spins out of control and later you have a much bigger mess to deal with.

When it comes to your emotional intelligence, the heart matters. The brain matters. And what you decide to do with the heart and the brain—what risks you take, what changes you make—that's the stuff of courage.

Holistic emotional intelligence requires us to weave together the three strands in real situations and in real time.

Like Dorothy, you need all of them to reach Oz.

 ## 3.7 Put This Info to Work

Take a look at the questions outlined at the beginning of the chapter. Which of these questions do you find most applicable? Circle or highlight three or more.

→ When has a threat response been triggered in you? When have you unintentionally triggered a threat response in someone else? Write about what happened and what you might do differently next time.

→ What sources of information (or whose information) do you regularly fail to consider? Why?

→ Strengthening your open-mindedness, like any other skill, requires practice and correct technique.

DOWNLOAD:
EQ EXERCISES

For a collection of exercises and tools to help answer these questions and improve your EQ, visit our online resources page.

CHAPTER SUMMARY:
THREE THINGS TO REMEMBER

→ Emotional intelligence requires courage; it takes guts to move beyond yourself and shape your environment.

→ The first step to shaping your office environment is open-minded, non-judgmental listening, hearing your employees' obstacles and needs. With listening will come hard feedback. And hard feedback will require more courage, courage to not resort to fight-or-flight, but to tap into your community.

→ When responding to feedback, troubleshooting issues, or facing new goals, reaching out for advice from those you trust will turn down the fears in the emotional center of your brain, freeing you up to utilize your rational, problem-solving center, paving the way for success.

PART TWO
Agility

CHAPTER 4

How To Recognize Your Environment

When I travel all over the world to work with different companies, I hear myself saying one thing over and over again:

The environment can be dangerous.

When I say this, I'm not talking about climate change or some kind of "man versus nature" TV show. I'm saying that without emotional intelligence, the environment will most likely get the better of you. Why? Let's revisit the brain.

Remember, the brain has adapted slowly over time. Our environment—with its many inventions, advances in technology, and increased speed—continues to change rapidly. And our brain? It just can't keep up. Consider all the time humans have spent honing our fight-or-flight instinct and now think of how recently email was invented.

So what's an emotionally intelligent leader to do?

First, you must understand this simple fact: the environment is dangerous in the sense that it is changing so fast, it is physically impossible for our minds to keep up. Now dive deeper. What kind of environment are we talking about here? How would we categorize it and how does it move? Bring in the brain: what does the brain do to try to keep up? How does it respond? We'll talk about how considering these questions is a crucial component to becoming a more emotionally intelligent leader who figures out how to work in an challenging environment.

 ## VUCA is the New Four-Letter Word

Reach for your phone. How long did it take?

Chances are, it was sitting right next to you—or maybe you're even reading this *from* your phone. There are more distractions now, with constant access to internet, and more information and data than there ever has been. We're walking around on cognitive overload. So much is vying for our attention. Around the time of the Cold War, the US military coined a term to explain climates of unpredictable and tumultuous events—and it's applicable now in the business world.[36] They used an acronym to describe it: VUCA. It stands for volatility, uncertainty, complexity, and ambiguity.

We have more data and knowledge now, but we also have significant and rapid changes in technology and customer expectations. So we're left with an environment that is hard to predict.

As Ira Wolfe explains in his book *Recruiting in the Age of Googlization:*[37]

V	**Volatility** is "turbulence; it's the nature, speed, volume and magnitude of change."
U	**Uncertainty** "relates to the lack of predictable issues and events."
C	**Complexity** "represents the difficult-to-understand causes and mitigating factors involved."
A	**Ambiguity** is "unknown unknowns, the haziness of reality" and "mixed meanings."

Where does this leave us?

In an environment that is turbulent, unpredictable, multi-factored, and foggy. **We live in a world where you need to keep on your toes. And while you're up there, it feels like you could be knocked over.** That's where emotional intelligence comes in.

In a VUCA situation, the brain will try to take shortcuts every chance it can; it will pursue the problems that are easiest to solve.

For instance, checking emails. We'll open up our email thinking we'll just take a peek—but what happens? An unpredictable, unexpected crisis sucks us in and the next thing we know, we spent time we could have spent on tackling big picture, high value problems or creating a strategy for a new project. Instead, two hours have passed without much to show for it. Your brain will naturally choose small, easy distractions over analytical, strategic, or creative thinking, because it's easier. Your environment tends to enable your brain, encouraging you to pursue easily gratified, less strenuous, and **often less important** tasks.

Knowing and recognizing this—ideally *while* it's happening—*that's* emotional intelligence.

Emotionally intelligent leaders recognize that VUCA gets you stuck in the little picture and they adjust their strategies to focus on what really matters.

If we are not sensitive to our environments and simply react to them instead of adapting or working with them, we can't survive—not to mention thrive—in it.

In a VUCA environment, though, sometimes what's missing is the warning. Operating in a VUCA-driven world takes awareness. It means recognizing that things change—and fast. What you came up with three minutes ago may not work now. We need to be sensitive to the way our environments are constantly changing and shaping new emotional responses in our teams. We have to create the infrastructure as leaders to prepare and adapt for the changes ahead. How you prepare your team matters. What you do to create trust and improve collaboration and communication are the things emotionally intelligent leaders do to survive, and even thrive, in the storm of VUCA.

The Difference Between Problems and Dilemmas

Is this a problem? Or is this a dilemma?

A problem is something that can be solved.

There's a way to come to a resolution and it's usually based on experience and expertise. You identify the problem, wrap your head around it, and you or a small group of people find a solution. For example a problem, in the case of one of my clients, was deciding which core system to use. They isolated the problem, analyzed their options, eliminated uncertainty by getting more information, and made a decision. They then acted on their decision with speed, and their core system was soon up and running.

Dilemmas, on the other hand, cannot be solved.

In an environment that creates always-moving targets, dilemmas are the targets. You can hit it, but it will move again.

Dilemmas can only be managed. There's no way to end a dilemma.

Dilemmas are messy and complicated and they involve many different sectors. Handling dilemmas is like surfing. You keep trying to catch the perfect wave, but can't seem to hold on to it—and you're never sure when you're going to wipe out. As Bob Johansen, a researcher at the Institute for the Future says, "We're moving from a world of problems to a world of continuous dilemmas."

Thrilling, right?

Not for the brain.

That's why emotional intelligence—which involves knowing how the brain is likely to respond to dilemmas and other challenges—becomes so essential.

JOT IT DOWN:

→ Set a timer for 90 seconds. Think and write:

When was the last time you encountered a

challenge at work?

What was it?

How did you address it?

Is it resolved or is it still outstanding?

Do you anticipate it coming back again, but in a

different iteration?

If it can be resolved, it's a problem. If it's going to

evolve and come back to you, it's a dilemma.

The key to managing dilemmas is to be careful not to judge too quickly or decide too late.

4.3 Case Study

A high tech firm I recently started working with found themselves managing the dilemma of their market shifting. They saw indications of it happening a year ago but fell into the trap of deciding too late. The global teams continued to want more data before acting; they wanted more clarity from the CEO and the senior team. The CEO and execs thought they had time. They weren't convinced the market would shift that fast. They thought it was a problem that could be solved and they thought they had three years to solve it. They didn't. The market shifted within months, not years. The consequence was massive layoffs. Their future is still unfolding and their success will depend on the CEO's ability to manage his own need for certainty, be willing to test and fail, and remain unafraid to make tough decisions. He will have to manage and adapt along the way. Not an easy task, but one that will be essential to spot the opportunities as they appear.

Emotional intelligence allows us to see the difference between problems and dilemmas and respond accordingly. In the case of dilemmas, highly emotionally intelligent leaders will refuse to get stuck because they're able to turn down the limbic brain that responds to fear with fight-or-flight and turn up their ability to creatively problem solve—including creatively designing an environment for them and their team.

The best leaders see dilemmas as opportunities for innovation.

They engage in what Bob Johansen calls "dilemma flipping," which he describes as "reframing an unsolvable challenge as an opportunity."[39] For instance, Disney World faced the dilemma of long lines at their amusement parks. It wasn't fixable—but the negative effect of the lines could be mitigated. They decided to address the dilemma by providing video entertainment, wait-time indicators, and even an app for visitors to interact with while they wait.[40]

Johansen's "dilemma flipping" helps us reassess our judgments. A more powerful perception-shifting strategy, pioneered by Edward de Bono as "lateral thinking", finds novel solutions which otherwise would never have been considered.[41] As de Bono explains: "Most of the mistakes in thinking are inadequacies of perception rather than mistakes of logic." Perception-shifting is a vital skill in the VUCA environment.

The Real Secret to Managing VUCA

There is no antidote to VUCA. The nature of VUCA, and the nature of the dilemma (rather than the problem), means *there is no cure*. There is only treatment. The good news is this: the treatment is accessible, renewable, and something you can improve upon with practice—it's your own emotional intelligence.

In the face of this volatile, uncertain, complex, and ambiguous climate, emotional intelligence gives us the insight to know why we are responding and how our reaction or response might be impacting others.

It's more important now, more than ever, for leaders to understand their own relational and situational triggers for anger, frustration, and shame. Self-awareness about *how we're responding to our environments* can help us avoid unnecessary conflicts and emotional outbursts. If we practice seeing and labeling emotions as they're happening, we feel less attached to them, which means we can respond in a way that's less reactive.

4.5 ## Put This Info to Work

→ Certainty in this VUCA environment will be dangerous, but emotionally intelligent leaders will have clarity. Rigid rules can create trouble in the VUCA world, while stories encourage people to engage and provide clarity.[42] What are the stories and the rules of your organization?

→ Know that you don't know it all. It's your job to look at the big picture, but know that the picture can shift and grow as you fill in the details. It's not only poor leadership to think you can know it all, but it's unreasonable.

→ Create conditions to experiment. MIT's research identified experimentation as the biggest hurdle companies face in a digital world. Train your brain for this VUCA world by experimenting and practicing. Immerse yourself in learning in new environments. Create platforms to experiment with new ideas. Recognize and reward employees for testing new ideas even if they fail. One company created internal software that mimicked the stock market to collect innovative ideas. Each idea received a stock ticker and employees could vote or buy stock in the ideas. Senior leaders could then see which ideas had the most traction.[43]

They found a fun and playful way to engage their organization in brainstorming.

→

→ Create a growth mindset culture. This will be critical in this new VUCA world where we're asking employees to take more risk with innovating. Have conversations around what failure looks like, how you can allow for certain types of failure, and use failure to grow. Keep conversations about failure positive and part of a learning context, otherwise employees may fail to innovate because the threat of failure will be too strong.

**CHAPTER SUMMARY:
THREE THINGS TO REMEMBER**

→ Emotionally intelligent leaders understand that the corporate sector, work environments, and technology are changing so fast it is physically impossible for our minds to keep up.

→ The current corporate landscape can best be described by the acronym VUCA: volatile, uncertain, complex, and ambiguous. These conditions naturally trigger fight-or-flight responses in leaders and employees alike.

→ Emotionally intelligent leaders identify when they are being triggered and work to respond quickly to changing markets, viewing dilemmas not as obstacles, but as opportunities for innovation.

CHAPTER 5

How To Increase Your Agility

Adapt or die. That's the environment we're in right now. That's what we're up against when volatility, uncertainty, complexity, and ambiguity (VUCA) are the water we swim in. As leaders, we have a choice: we can allow our environments to control us, or we can take back control and design our environments to optimize our brains.

You can take back control and design your environments by both being agile and creating an agile workplace.

How does agility connect to EQ? Researchers Peter Salovey and John D. Meyer defined agility in their unprecedented research as "the subset of social intelligence that involves the ability to monitor one's own and others' feelings and emotions, to discriminate among them, and to use this information to guide one's thinking and actions."[44]

Agility is having the confidence to look to the uncertain future and remain willing to anticipate risks, take risks, execute quickly, and course-correct as needed.

These course corrections will happen often as you constantly monitor the current environment and the future environment. Agility means you connect the dots and form a hypothesis and then test that hypothesis. It requires confidence to move when it's uncertain, and it requires humility and vulnerability to admit the need to change directions and correct accordingly.

In my experience, retaining humility and vulnerability is the most difficult part for leaders. Have you ever seen someone so set on their course that they have a hard time admitting when it's not working? Have you seen them defend their course at all costs?

"What the human being is best at doing is interpreting all new information so that their prior conclusions remain intact."

-Warren Buffett

The most common derailer of agility is defending— remaining closed or defensive when challenged.[45] Agility demands the emotional intelligence to know when to put ego aside and let go of proving you're right. Agile individuals and teams are able to discard perspectives, ideas, and skills that are no longer relevant.[46]

5.1 The EQ³ Advantage

In Part I, we talked about how holistic emotional intelligence involves recognizing the *we*, not just the *me*, and then adapting your environment to support the self and relationships. Let's talk about the effect of adding agility to the mix:

→ **ENVIRONMENT**
Having agile emotional intelligence means maintaining the ability to recognize and understand what kind of emotional response is best suited for the environment. It means you are strong enough to challenge the status quo, willing

to adapt to the changing needs, and you have the confidence to learn key lessons from your failures. You work toward maintaining the relationships between yourself and others who share your environment.

→ RELATIONSHIPS

An agile emotional intelligence in relationships means you can trust that you're able to correctly read a person's mood. You can challenge or sway the mood of the room and people in it. You also are wise enough to realize you don't have all the answers. So you ask for help, utilize the talents of others, and work together without feeling threatened by what others can do.

→ SELF

You have intrinsic value that is not undercut when it comes time to ask for support. You have the ability to leverage networks. When challenging decisions you have the courage to manage the emotional reactions and fears of others to make a tough call that is good for the whole team. When mistakes occur, you choose to course correct rather than nurse a bruised ego. You know that one interaction, one instance, or even one person's opinion, doesn't define you.

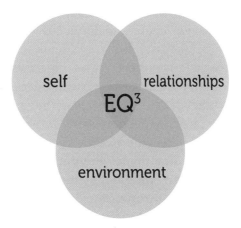

When we do not set up our environments to be agile, we work *against our brain* and are at the mercy of fear. We need to be on the lookout against consistent cognitive overload and distraction.

→ **AWARENESS**
Part of being agile is recognizing what drains us. Daily distractions are so ubiquitous, it's like driving on a road that has more potholes than pavement. This puts us in what researchers call "continuous partial attention"—a state that leads to constant stress. And when we're stressed, we engage the fight-or-flight response more easily.[47]

Here's the pattern: we think if we stretch ourselves more and more, we'll get more done. But we don't. We become dumber (because our attention is split) and our decision-making suffers. We become mentally exhausted. Then we start feeling bad about ourselves. We think "I didn't get to this," or "I wasn't able to get to that." We walk into the meeting even more stressed. And the cycle repeats. **This vicious cycle creates the condition to significantly lower your emotional intelligence. We can combat it by maintaining agile relationships and environments. Incorporating agility is essential to not just survive, but thrive.**

5.2 Case Study: How to Drive Real Change

I was working with Brad, a CEO who was so far from thriving that he was struggling to survive. The stress of the job was triggering his limbic brain to signal fight-or-flight. He'd become angry and frustrated with his environment. Revenue was down, vendors were becoming unpredictable, markets were shifting, customers were becoming more demanding and harder to understand. His emotional state was anger, frustration, fear, and uncertainty.

How did this manifest? He was yelling at his executives and boiling over in meetings. He would scream at people for their mistakes. And as he was combusting, the trust of his organization was plummeting and the psychological safety of his teams was tanking. He was laying out the conditions that create fear and a lack of trust and therefore a lack of willingness to bring up new ideas, issues, or failures. The company was in meltdown mode.

When I started to work with the company, the first thing we had to do was get to the root of the problem, which I quickly realized was fear. After probing deeper into the problem with me, Brad was able to recognize that he was angry because the solutions he'd used in the past were no longer working and he didn't understand why. He was worried. What if he failed? He was in the fight response.

After helping Brad examine his current emotional state by creating distance, he began to calm down and recognize there was an opportunity in the changing environment—he had just been too busy fuming and burning bridges to see it.

"It is not the logical part of thinking that changes emotions, but the perceptual part. If we see something differently, our emotions may alter with the altered perception."[48]

I encouraged Brad to reach out to his peer groups and get a sense of the issues they were dealing with and how they were addressing them. When he learned they were dealing with similar dilemmas in volatile foreign markets, he was not only able to learn from them but also felt a bit assured—this was happening to them, too. He wasn't alone in it. He could start to see it was the environment beyond his company—the marketplace around him and the consumer expectations—that was causing his crisis, not just his team.

Over the course of a month, Brad began calmly addressing his teams. He asked people to bring ideas to the table and then he validated those ideas. He addressed the failures that had happened internally. He told his employees that moving forward, he was going to address failure differently than he had been. Instead of yelling, he was going to focus on experimenting and learning from their mistakes.

And then? He really did adapt. He started to change the environment that he could control. He put project-learning teams together responsible for experimenting with new ideas. He gave those team leaders decision-making authority. Together, Brad and his team leaders made it safe to fail within these project-learning teams because no one would be punished for failure. They would only take their failures and turn them into key lessons.

Within the unsteady waters of the environment, a shift began to take place. The company became more agile and more creative. Based on their trials and learnings, they found some market opportunities that led to an increased $300,000 in revenue per month.

It took agility on all three levels—self, relationships, and environment—to turn the ship around. But the company was able to do it. And if a leader is willing to grow their emotional intelligence, it can be seen in the bottom line.

Understanding the factors that trigger fight-or-flight—the fear that made that CEO so combustible—and the emotions associated with the triggers allows us to spot when we are experiencing an emotion. We're not reacting to a lion in the woods anymore. We're reacting to complex problems that need us to engage our rational prefrontal cortex instead of our emotional limbic brain.

Observing our impulse to react emotionally allows us to label and reframe. Without agile self-awareness, you will not be able to adapt and direct your behavior. You need to take note of your emotions as they happen, in real time.

Being able to regulate yourself is central to building agile relationships and environments.

If you can't label the emotion, the emotion will label you—and you'll become known as the angry leader or the leader who sticks their head in the sand—not the leader who was able to take anger, fear, and threats, and turn them into opportunities.

Four Tips to Navigate the (Mental) Agility Course

Like a physical agility course, it helps to have routes set up for your mind. Think of it as jumping tires or climbing ropes—but for the brain. If you have a route *already set up,* then you will train your mind to go through these agility building steps, and soon it will be part of your routine.

Tip 1 **CREATE SPACE FOR HIGHER-LEVEL THINKING.**

Appreciate and respect that your prefrontal cortex is a limited resource. When your brain is the most fresh, usually in the morning, use that time well by turning off your phone and email and focusing on more complex thinking such as setting priorities, thinking strategically or creatively, or complex problem-solving.

Tip 2 **DECIDE WHAT DECISIONS NEED TO BE MADE.**

The most energy-sucking task the brain has to do is prioritize and make complex decisions. President Obama only wore blue or gray suits because he wanted to focus his decision-making energy elsewhere.[50] Figure out what you need to decide on and what you can delegate or put on autopilot. I know when I hit decision fatigue and I will consciously not make decisions until the following morning when I'm refreshed.

Tip 3 **SEQUENCE YOUR DECISIONS.**

I worked with a vice president of a company who was struggling with decisions that were keeping her up at night. But she was often worrying about decisions that she couldn't even make yet because she didn't yet have the necessary information. I told her to write down all the decisions that needed to be made and then put them in order based on when they needed to be done. This allowed her to address those pesky unresolved issues and decipher which issues were taking up space in the brain, creating emotional havoc, but couldn't be decided yet.

Tip 4 **SURROUND YOURSELF WITH HONESTY (EVEN IF IT'S UNCOMFORTABLE).**

Get advice from people who are willing to be honest and aren't worried about hurting your feelings. I love the people in my life who are willing to do that for me. I reached out to a colleague when I was writing this book and asked for his thoughts on the structure. He said he didn't like it at all, which sparked me to make some important changes. People in my life who are willing to tell me the hard things are so rare and valuable.

> *"The extent to which an individual or group can cycle quickly through these cognitive and emotional processing activities will shape their success with rapid decision-making."*
>
> *- Institute or the Future[51]*

5.4 The Importance of Agility

Our ancestors had to think about actual survival, like escaping a bear, rather than social survival. They would have to respond without analytical thinking and simply listen to their emotions telling them to escape. We're now in an environment where responding purely with emotion, without the reason and analytical thinking provided by the prefrontal cortex, causes harm. Agile emotional intelligence manages the fight-or-flight response, limits distractions, and calls into focus higher-order thinking.

The prefrontal cortex is a limited resource. Agility means you can stretch that resource, but you can't stretch it by splitting its attention. You can stretch it by understanding its limited nature and prioritizing accordingly. Limited resource settings call for agility.

So set up your work, your decisions, and your day to get the most out of a very critical and limited resource. Don't waste it on responding to emails or draining yourself first with unimportant tasks. Limit distractions when you have to do complex or creative thinking. Turn everything off and focus. Then see where your agility takes you.

How to Improve Your Agility

→ What new and unique ideas can you and your team come up with? How can you look at your initiatives or problems from different angles? How can you challenge the status quo?

→ What new skills can you add to remain agile?

→ How can you stretch yourself and take more calculated risks?

→ What can you observe about what is happening in your environment? Where do you need to listen more to learn?

→ What feedback can you get to determine what assumptions you're holding that may or may not be true?

DOWNLOAD:
AGILITY EXERCISES

For a collection of exercises and tools to help you improve your agility, visit our online resources page.

**CHAPTER SUMMARY:
THREE THINGS TO REMEMBER**

→ Agility is having the confidence to look to the future, knowing it's uncertain, and remain willing to anticipate risks, take risks, execute quickly, and course-correct as needed.

→ Being able to detect and label thoughts, fears, and emotions is essential in exercising agility.

→ Labeling sets you up to regulate yourself, manage your fight-or-flight response, and maximize your ability to execute strategic risks.

PART THREE

Relationships

CHAPTER 6

Understanding Team Dysfunction

To drill down to the *why*, you need the emotional intelligence to address the "same old, same old" that throws you off course. You need to see the common barriers as detours.

But even after you figure out the *why* and you bring intelligence about emotion into your leadership, there are winds that will blow you off course—things that will throw you off the track. **These are what I call derailers.**

Derailers are those "dysfunctional interpersonal and self-regulatory patterns that interfere with the leader's capacity to build and maintain high-performing teams."[52]

Derailers will corrupt the leader's skills, experience, and intelligence and stop them from leveraging their strengths.

When do derailers most tend to emerge? You guessed it: in volatile, uncertain, complex, and ambiguous situations. It's VUCA again—because in today's day and age, VUCA just won't quit.

Derailers prefer to emerge in times of stress, high emotion, ambiguity, and exhaustion. Why? Because that's when we're most vulnerable.

And to combat these derailers, you again need the intelligent use of emotion to right your course. In Part III of this book, we'll talk about relationships— with yourself, others, and your environment—and how EQ³ can help leverage motivation in all of these relationships.

Emotional intelligence is not a cure-all, but it can help you address the common challenges and barriers that would otherwise hold you back. Intelligently addressing our emotions helps us rise above our flawed views of ourselves and others and lead with self-awareness, social intelligence, and environmental sensitivity. You've got to know your own derailers and get to the *why* behind them. Everyone faces some kind of potential derailer. The question is whether you have the emotional intelligence to right your course.

How We Derail Ourselves from Success

How often have you heard that to get better, you should focus on your strengths?

But it is not your strengths that cause you to derail. Of course not. It's your derailers that throw you off track. In my work, I've seen more substantial gains—in leadership, trust, and profitability—when leaders decide to tackle their derailers. They focus on understanding and addressing what throws them off track.

For instance, let's say you have an important strategy session because the market is demanding your business model to shift. The wise thing to do would be to move into creative problem-solving mode, which happens in the prefrontal cortex, but it's hard to make the leap because of the fear of failing. What if your ideas don't work out?

So your limbic brain avoids the problem. That's a derailer.

In avoidance, you become your own worst enemy. You continue to focus on maintaining and improving your current operations as you avoid and ignore.

The odds will be better if you try to focus on maintaining your current state, rather than risk failure by trying something new—or so you think. You have become your own villain.

You and your team don't achieve the innovation your business needs, and innovation initiatives fail or stall, as does your reputation as a leader. This makes the situation become even more threatening, so you turn the avoidance up a notch (or three). One bad decision leads to another. You miss several opportunities to reach out and get help from leadership. It becomes clear to others that you had succeeded in the past by operating in your safe domain that you were familiar with. But now you're struggling with ambiguity. You start feeling down on yourself and wondering why you're not doing better professionally. Maybe avoidance even creeps into your personal relationships. How did you get here?

In your fear of risk, you've missed the opportunities because your brain is focused on the threat. It's focusing on how and why you might fail. **You have derailed yourself.**

These impulses are what I call derailers, but we could also think of them as villains. They're the impulses inside each of us that served us well at one point in time but now hold us back. Maybe avoiding conflict at home as a child was beneficial. Maybe blaming someone else got you out of trouble in your family. Maybe striving for perfectionism helped you achieve what you didn't think you could. But these are also impulses that, left unchecked, will throw us completely off course.

If we don't do the work
of knowing our derailers,
it's like trying to drive with
the parking brake still on:
you can try to accelerate,
but you are wasting a lot
of effort.

Derailers live in the limbic brain and are born in
childhood—our brain is trying to keep us alive
into adulthood. It adopts habits in order to survive.
Dysfunctional interpersonal behaviors often reflect
distorted beliefs and flawed mental models a leader may
have about themselves and others in the environment.
Fears of failure, inadequacy, and rejection can cloud the
leader's judgment and impair interactions with direct
reports and peers.[53]

The fight-or-flight response initiates your derailers. The
emotional center of our brains, the limbic system, pulls
the strings. It's as if we're Pinocchio, allowing the limbic

brain to pull the strings. We might be *aware* of Jiminy Cricket, that wise prefrontal cortex talking—that voice of *reason*—but until we learn to recognize that we're being pulled by our own strings, and figure out how to free ourselves from them (even just temporarily), we'll never be able to act on the wise voice of the cricket.

6.2 The Six Common Derailers

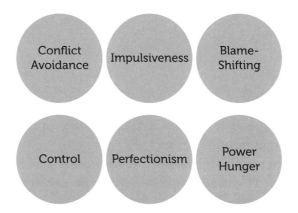

So, what are the puppet strings held by your limbic brain? How do the fears kick into action and run the show? The things that hold us back are surprisingly common, but that doesn't make them easy to address.

1. CONFLICT AVOIDANCE

Using escape or intimidation to mask insecurities.

This is when you avoid making decisions to dodge criticism and find it hard to get out of your comfort zone. Leaders who avoid conflict often pay the price because the conflict comes out as passive aggressive behavior or highly volatile emotions.

High EQ Response: Recognize the fear that's making you avoid the challenge is the same fear that's going to get you in trouble later. Once you label your driver as "fear," it becomes easier to face. Seek advice on how to confront the conflict, issue, or challenge. If you're nervous, start by simply writing down your plan. It's best if you can respond to the situation directly and in person.

2. IMPULSIVENESS

The degree to which a person can control the need for immediate gratification.

This is when you act on the limbic brain's impulses and it often takes you to a place you didn't intend. You may alienate others through unpredictable emotional responses such as anger and frustration. When you fall into the habit of impulsiveness you lose relationships, support, and buy-in.

High EQ Response: True learning requires building on previous knowledge, successes, and failures. Take time to reflect on previous decisions and what "clues" were there, but were missed. For future projects, anticipate consequences by asking a series of problem questions such as:

→ What is most likely to fail in execution?

→ What have I missed?

→ How will this be perceived by others inside and outside the organization?

3. BLAME-SHIFTING

This is a bias toward exaggerating the negative and feeling like a victim.

This is when you mask insecurities by placing the problem on someone else. It's a sense of "poor me," or "it's someone else's fault," be it a department, management, or something else. Blame-shifting often causes others to disengage because they get tired of hearing it.

This is the most common derailer I see in the corporate world. Our company uses psychometrics to measure derailers and blame-shifting is the number one cause of poor problem-solving and lack of innovation.

High EQ Response: Identify the assumptions that come with rationalizing blame-shifting. These are the three common assumptions that make blame-shifting feel okay:

→ When you assume you are faultless, you rationalize that you should not be blamed.

→ When you assume that you are powerless, you rationalize that you have no control and so should not be blamed.

→ When you assume someone is bad or mean, then you rationalize that it is okay to blame them.

Once you are free from the trap of these assumptions, you can admit that you are not faultless, you are not powerless, and others do things without evil intent. These three acknowledgments allow you to admit your failures, take action, and build relationships with others.

4. CONTROL

This is the desire to exert authority, potentially leading you to be perceived as rigid and a micromanager.

This is when you seize control to avoid failure. Ironically, when you act on this fear, you exhibit behaviors that cause those around you to shut down. Employees working for a controlling leader stop taking initiative, they no longer offer up ideas, and avoid giving valuable feedback.

High EQ Response: Share the goal and its metrics and recruit the team to help. In this way, the desired outcome and potential threats are shared and managed by an engaged team. The distribution of control prevents you from becoming a roadblock and allows your team to ensure the success.

5. PERFECTIONISM

This tendency is when you work hard to make things perfect, but chasing this dream means you may miss deadlines or opportunities.

This is when you're too busy imagining how things could have been to appreciate where they are now. I've witnessed perfectionism so extreme that a person fails to submit their work simply because it didn't meet their standards of perfection.

High EQ Response: Get confirmation on standards. Often perfectionists set unrealistically high standards, so seek feedback on expected results, costs, and timelines to get a reality check. Try small experiments of relaxing your standards slightly. What happened? Were your worst fears realized? Challenge your own thoughts about expectations. Are they logical and reasonable? How does your perfectionism impact your relationships? The need to always be right will often annoy others and in extreme cases drive others away.

6. POWER HUNGER

Power is defined as "asymmetric control over valued resources in a social relationship,"[54] and this is when you claim too much of it.

As a power hungry leader, you tend to keep a laser focus on your own goals; you can "discount the needs of others, be less willing to compromise, and rely on mental shortcuts and stereotypes when you make decisions."[55] You see others as a means to an end. Lack of empathy, failure to see risks, and a tendency to make snap decisions can be a deadly combination—and costly for an organization.[56] Power hungry leaders alienate the hearts and minds of those around them.

High EQ Response: Research shows that leaders with a strong moral identity and sense of responsibility to others used their power for good and that power inspired them to be more selfless.[57]

Create policies and systems to hold leaders accountable for their behavior. "One way to increase perspective-taking in the powerful is through accountability," says power researcher, Adam Galinksy. Share power by engaging individuals around their strengths. Recruiting a team's motivation, perspective, and expertise multiplies power and distributes it to meet the demands of the VUCA environment.

 ## 6.3 We're Not as Self-Aware as We Think

Take a minute and look again over the list of common derailers. Which of these have you experienced at one point or another? Can you think of a scenario in your life where these derailers might affect you?

It might be easier to recognize the derailers in others, but highly emotionally intelligent people have learned to also recognize them within themselves. Doing this isn't easy.

In his book *Triggers,* Dr. Marshall Goldsmith reports on a study that shows just how terribly unaware many of us are.

In a study of more than 80,000 professionals, 70% believed they were in the top 10% of their peer group.

Let that sink in.

Then, there's this: 82% believed they were in the top 20% of their peer group and 98.5% believed they were in the top half.

Take one more look at that list while thinking about your own tendencies and the scenarios or circumstances in which they might arise...

As Goldsmith explains, almost all of us have a habit of crediting ourselves and blaming others or situations (even if we think we don't).

To prevent these derailing habits, it's essential to know the triggers that will set you off. These might be situations, comments from others, or interactions with certain content or messaging.

How can you recognize the tendencies we've just listed? It takes work and practice. First, consider which derailers you tend toward, and in what kinds of scenarios. Maybe when there's pressure with a project, you lean toward perfectionism and if there's pressure with people, you lean toward conflict avoidance.

"Derailed managers typically cost their companies more

than 150% of their annual salary."[58]

Ask yourself:

→ What people or situations influence the quality of my performance? Think of a specific example.

→ What emotion did I experience right before the trigger?

→ Did the trigger change my emotional state?

→ What was my impulse or reaction? Is that my normal reaction to that trigger?

→ What behavior resulted from my reaction?

→ What outcome did it create for me and others?

Determine if it's positive or counterproductive. These triggers are only an issue if your response to the trigger creates a problem. The pressure of a new project is only a problem if my response is to become overly perfectionistic and demanding, which demotivates my team, lowers productivity, and increases the chance of missing our deadline.

When I feel the need to step in and over-manage, I ask myself about this impulse: Is this coming from the idea that *no one else can do it like me*? Technically this is true, but what I have often found is that, like in the case of my assistant, she can often do things better than I can once I explain what I'm trying to achieve. It just takes coaching, time, and feedback. I have to be willing to delay the instant gratification of getting it done faster myself, for the longer term benefit of equipping my team to be able to do it on their own. And as a consequence of me taking the time to do those things, my team can really flourish.

How to Recognize Derailers in Others

Derailers within ourselves can be hard to see and hard to change, but what about when you see someone else derail?

What can you do when you recognize derailers in your employees?

→ Talk to them about the ways derailers can limit their progress.

→ Figure out how they view themselves, and how others view them, and help them understand the difference.

→ Help them understand that their strengths can't compensate for their derailers, so they need to work on their derailers.

What can you do to mitigate the effects of other people's derailers on you?

Sometimes you're not in a position to address the derailers of others. What then? The next best thing is to work to mitigate their impact on you.

→ Remember you have options in how you respond.

→ Practice not taking it personally by changing the focus to view from their perspective. What are they trying to convey? Maybe they don't have great social skills. We have a natural tendency to make things more negative and personal than they really are.[59]

→ Begin to recognize the triggers that set off their derailing tendencies. Does it often happen with certain projects, people, or situations? Have a conversation with them. For example, if they're micromanaging you can say, "The outcome of this project is clearly important to you. What concerns you most about it?" Seek to understand. Once you understand, you will likely be able to come to a solution on how to address it in a healthier way.

→ Imagine their past and how they may have grown up. This exercise helps to cultivate your compassion toward them, enabling you to view them and their derailers as less threatening.

6.5 Case Study: Meeting the Challenge of Identifying Your Derailers

Derailers are crucial for two reasons—one, because you can't begin to think about a group or a system without recognizing them and where they are manifesting, and two, because sometimes your own derailers are the only things you *can* control in a situation. Yet we know from earlier chapters that addressing the *me* is only half of emotional intelligence: **we have to also address the *we*.**

The most common derailer of a group, environment, or system is blame-shifting.

It's easy to sit back and judge other people. Usually, it's far easier for us to place blame on others than it is to look inward at our own derailers.

Recently, I was working with a high tech company on the west coast. The business model of this firm's clients was shifting, and it was cause for them to change, too. Up until this point, what they've been doing has worked. They have high revenue, a great reputation, and decades of experience. They want to keep doing well— really, really well. But doing so requires innovation.

So, what do these new demands do to their system? They have to maintain and improve their current system *while* they innovate. This, we know from earlier, creates a challenge. The limbic brain wants something low risk and is content with small improvements. Innovation is a big risk and will likely involve a lot of failure—it's very possible that only one out of ten of their new strategic initiatives will work.

To help make this leap, the company hired a marketing data analytics firm to analyze their market and present on their results. In a nutshell, the marketing firm presented a significant amount of data and came to this conclusion: *you have a solid, trusted brand and the conditions are favorable to introducing new products and services*. The marketers had surveyed their clients and learned that the clients would be interested in the new products.

What do you think happened?

If you guessed they were still hesitant, you're right. Despite the data, despite the reason, fear was still holding this team back. They questioned the data the marketing firm presented, and not in just a healthy way, but in a defensive way. They were worried.

After the presentation, we discussed what happened. "You have a trusted brand," I said. "You've been tremendously successful. Last year, you all met and talked about the need to innovate. What initiatives did you execute in the past year?"

There were crickets. Nada. Their derailer was exposed: the fear of uncertainty.

"Now it's time to change and innovate," I said, "and when presented with the most analytic data you could find, you argued with it. Is this data 100% sure? Of course not. Innovation is never 100% sure. But waiting for 100% certainty is holding you back from moving forward."

For this company, there were several derailers in play. First and foremost, the fear of uncertainty caused the company to avoid what needed to be addressed. Still, they managed to get past this by hiring the marketing firm. During the presentation, they picked at the data— could this other factor account for the change? Had the marketers considered X, Y, and Z? These were signs of the control and perfectionism derailers. I listened as they blamed the market, their clients for changing and not showing loyalty to them, and they blamed the CEO for not providing enough clarity on what and how to innovate. And throughout all of it, there was the fear of failure that comes with risk: What if we get it wrong? Will it cost us our jobs, our reputation, our profit?

These are important questions to ask and important aspects to consider, but **letting derailers make the decision for you is not only unwise, it's dangerous.**

The challenge of emotional intelligence is to recognize these concerns—which are rooted in emotion, not logic—and then decide whether to act in response to them or not.

The firm was reluctant to change, but decided to try. Once we revealed the root cause of their hesitation, the team began to see what they needed to do. You see, your derailer loses some of its power when it is revealed. One leader even laughed and said, "It's like we've all been standing on this starting line for the past year, looking up and down the line wondering who will go first. And we're all still standing here."

Now they're ready to band together and take one giant step forward.

6.6 The Importance of Being Self-Aware

If a stranger were to inform us that we had bad breath and then offer us a mint, I think most of us would probably take it and thank them. But it's funny how if that same stranger told us we were arrogant, most of us would more than likely decline the proffered piece of humble pie. No thanks.

It's an odd juxtaposition because bad breath is simply unpleasant, while arrogance is a career killer.

95% of us think we're self-aware, **but in reality, only** 10–15% of us truly are.[60]

When I meet with teams that are low in trust, often the most senior leader is the least aware of how he or she affects the emotions and behavior of those seated nearby. In low-trust teams, the leader who asks for candor rarely gets it. The uncertainty of the VUCA environment extends to the uncertainty between people and the weak spots in their relationships. And we know this about VUCA, it can create its own perfect storm.

Surviving office politics tempts us to defensively guard our reputation at all costs. Most of us do this by building up layers of protective ego-saving armor. Wearing our ego armor is both awkward and burdensome, and it makes for rather cold metallic handshakes. But it saves us from the admission that, underneath, we are all quite human.

What if, instead of avoiding, ignoring, blaming, controlling, perfecting, or generally just *being afraid*, you honed your emotional intelligence?

Studying our own derailers helps us identify how we act, and how those actions prevent us from reaching our goals—whether they're career-oriented, social, or physical. Examining how we're acting allows us to get to the root of our behavior and see what thought, feeling, or circumstance has acted as a catalyst and set the derailing behavior or thought pattern into motion.

Awareness of our triggers can help us either avoid them or increase our awareness when we are interacting with them. **We can then meet our derailers with both compassion and accountability.**

How to avoid derailing: **When a threat is activated in the body, you only have a few seconds to respond.** This isn't an exaggeration—you really only have the few seconds it takes for the oxygen and glucose to move from the prefrontal cortex, where they help with analysis, to the limbic center, where they respond to fear in emotionally unintelligent ways. This is just how the brain works.

But you can do something. You can craft a plan. And when I say *craft a plan*, I mean really sit down and think about or write about it. You have to think about how you'll handle your derailer popping up, so when it does, you can easily recall the plan from memory rather than react emotionally.

I have scripts (however brief) to memorize and use during those critical times. You can check them out by going online to see the "Squirrel-Wrangling Scripts." In doing this, you don't have to think or reason (which can be difficult in a VUCA environment); you can just jump right into the script you've already created. I've helped my clients create scripts for the times they know they may get into trouble—when their emotions are most likely to get the best of them.

VISIT ONLINE RESOURCES TO:

Download targeted scripts to handle derailers.

Derailers limit our emotional freedom. Dr. Paul Ekman, the world's deception detection expert explains, **"The earlier you recognize an emotion, the more choice you will have in dealing with it. In Buddhist terms, it's recognizing the spark before the flame. In Western terms, it's trying to increase the gap between impulse and saying or doing something you might regret later."**[61]

6.7 How to Adopt A Growth Mindset

This type of recognition, use of a script, and reaction plan are similar to elements of what Carol Dweck, a psychology professor at Stanford University, has called the "growth mindset."[62] Dr. Dweck has spent her career studying motivation, personality, and why people succeed, and her research has led her to identify **two types of mindsets, fixed and growth.**

People with fixed mindsets view talent as something they either do or do not have. People with growth mindsets believe that intelligence, skills, and abilities can be developed, and tend to enjoy challenges and strive continually to learn.[63]

We can use emotional intelligence, in its whole form—from *me* and *we* to *why*—to cultivate our growth mindset. Employees with growth mindsets are more likely to find their colleagues trustworthy and behave in a more ethical way, and organizations with growth mindsets are more innovative and collaborative. The growth mindset is the work of the prefrontal cortex, not the limbic system.

So cultivating a growth mindset means we have to learn to manage our emotional tendencies of control, blame, avoidance, and other derailers.

And it *almost* goes without saying, but I find it's important to remember we can only change if we really want to.

When it comes to your environment in the workplace, creating a growth mindset culture requires a multi-pronged approach. It must become a priority that's communicated by senior leadership, reinforcing positive habits such as feedback conversations and risk-taking, and through systems such as hiring and processes.

Communicate Messages	Reinforce Habits	Build Systems

6.8 How to Manage and Overcome Your Derailers

Grab a pen and paper.

→ Review each derailer again. Which ones do you identify with?

→ How is that derailer driving you? What negative thoughts surface? Anger, shame, fear of failing, judging yourself or others, fear of not being liked?

→ What lies do you tell yourself to justify your derailers?

→ Label your derailers to expose them. Create your own name for them and when one surfaces, simply note it and say, "There goes my derailer _____ again."

→ What would change in your life if your derailer was exposed and diminished?

→ Take back control and put yourself in the driver's seat by instead using positive emotions. Move into curiosity, awareness, and agility. What do you need to accept rather than judge, deny, or blame?

→ What's creating frustration or stress for you right now? How can you turn that into an opportunity? What's positive about it?

**CHAPTER SUMMARY:
THREE THINGS TO REMEMBER**

→ Derailers are "dysfunctional interpersonal and self-regulatory patterns" that corrupt leaders' skills, experience, and intelligence and prevent them from leveraging their strengths. Some of the most common derailers are conflict avoidance, impulsiveness, blame-shifting, control, perfectionism, and power hunger.

→ Derailers often emerge in times of stress, high emotion, ambiguity, and exhaustion. Emotionally intelligent leaders know the derailers they are prone to and know the triggers that set them off.

→ Addressing derailers head-on positions leaders to maximize their strengths, their employees' strengths, and their companies' opportunities for growth.

CHAPTER 7

How To Motivate Your Team (And Yourself)

Most researchers consider motivation to be one of the key dimensions of EQ. So far, we've talked about the ways our brains are hardwired to find safe and secure connections with others. We all have a desire for community, need a sense of security, and experience responses to fear—that's what we have in common. But motivation is something different. Once we meet our baseline social and physical security, we have time to think about the unique ways we are driven to perform.

Motivation is the driving force or the *why* behind your behavior. It includes your likes, dislikes, values, viewpoints, and interests that become consciously or subconsciously a standard for guiding your actions.

Motivation exerts a predictive force of cause and effect.

When we understand
the different kinds of
motivators, we can predict
the reaction: how people
will make decisions and
respond to social threats
and opportunities.

This chapter illustrates what *not* to do, the difference
between motivation and compliance, and how leaders
use emotional intelligence to leverage relationships and
drive motivation.

 ## 7.1 What Not To Do: Compliance And "The Carrot & The Stick"

Traditional wisdom dictates that people don't like to
work, and they will avoid it if they can. Leaders who
buy into this fallacy believe that in order to get people
to work, they need to coerce, control, command,

or threaten them—and they think these tactics are motivation. But they're not. Using these tactics, or "the stick," instead generate **compliance**: the act of conforming, acquiescing, or yielding.

Compliance is a response to extrinsic forces: an external motivation from a person of authority. Think of compliance as someone trying to bend you.

7.2 Why the Workplace Isn't Like a Carnival Game

Too often we treat the workplace like a carnival game. We throw balls at pins until we knock them down and receive a prize. Maybe it's a prize we want, and that we've been eyeing for a while–like a bonus or a benefit.

But if we miss the pins, we find out there's punishment instead of a prize. There are negative repercussions, punishment, probation, or some other step backward.

The problem with a management style that mimics a carnival is that work *isn't* a game. Work is not something you go to in order to pass the time. You're not just there for entertainment and fun.

Sure, there are times when work *can* be entertaining and fun. And I'm sure we've all had days when we felt like we're just passing the time. But by and large, the most successful workplaces use a different set of motivators than reward and punishment.

Sustained motivation is internal—it is the result of a person wanting to take an action or follow the rules. A motivated person meets or exceeds expectations because they want to, not because they're being bribed, commanded, or threatened.

Emotionally intelligent
leaders know how to
engage their employees
and unleash individual and
group motivation.

Let's go back to the carnival example to see where the
conventional wisdom is flawed. When you want the
prize, you try harder to knock down the pins. The drive
to perform well in a high-stakes situation where your
livelihood is at risk creates pressure. It becomes *very*
important to knock down those pins. This makes you a
more nervous pitcher. Maybe you perform well under
pressure or maybe you fold. Regardless, here's what you
need to know about creating *that* kind of pressure:

Motivation that comes from a threatening environment is *motivation to protect, not motivation to perform.*

Think about it—you're less likely to take risks, try something new, or be creative in your approach when failing means you might lose your livelihood. You focus instead on protecting what you have.

Sticks, in other words, keep us hopping and often demoralized.

As for carrots? They don't help much either.

 ## 7.3   Intrisic vs. Extrinsic Motivation

I have seen many managers throw compensation or bonuses at teams in attempts to motivate them to innovate. But they end up sabotaging their own goals, because in environments where there's an emphasis on extrinsic motivation, employees are afraid to lose and failure is high risk.

Another challenge that comes with using extrinsic motivators is that rewards and punishments can often backfire. Take the many examples of children being rewarded for activities they already enjoy, like drawing or reading. School districts pulled out of the infamous Pizza Hut reading program (where students earned free personal pan pizzas for reading a certain number of books) when teachers reported that, after enrolling in the program, reading comprehension levels and student satisfaction with reading had gone down.

Why? Because **extrinsic motivators can often unintentionally replace intrinsic motivators.**

Intrinsic motivation, doing something because it's personally rewarding to you, is uniquely different than extrinsic motivation, where the task is seen as a means to obtain something else or avoid punishment.

When we are given external bribes and prizes to read, we're less likely to enjoy the process of reading for reading's sake. Students still read books in the Pizza Hut program, but the books they chose were shorter and below their reading level because the book now became an obstacle to get their reward: the pizza.

Here's another example:

WHY EXTRINSIC MOTIVATORS SOMETIMES BACKFIRE

Consider the story of the daycare that began to fine parents who picked up their children late.[66] What happened? Late pickups increased significantly. The fine removed the intrinsic motivator of being considerate to the daycare staff who wanted to leave on time. Now people could just pay a fee and be late, which seemed far easier. The relationship component was made far more transactional.

 7.4

Why Smart Companies Don't Base Compensation on Employee Goals

Many big companies are decoupling goals and compensation. Google made the decision to separate goals from both performance reviews and compensation decisions.[67] This is because people are less likely to set ambitious goals–goals that require some risk–when their compensation is on the line.

Think about it: when the stakes are high, you're more likely to set easier-to-reach goals so that you can succeed. As a result, innovation suffers. Thus, the key is to reward employees for setting aggressive, challenging goals, without having compensation hinge on these goals. Sure, as a leader you need deliverables. As for what those should be, you can look toward operating plans when projects are more routine and there is high certainty. At Anheuser-Busch InBev, bonuses are linked to routine improvements. These include cost reductions, operational improvements, and optimizing pricing–their bread and butter.[68]

To encourage employees to learn and fail, on the other hand, they set other ambitious goals separate from compensation. You can do this by focusing on learning plans in situations where there is less certainty and more creativity is required.[69] Learning plans help test assumptions and assess gaps. Tying *all* of an employee's goals to their compensation will likely deter them from the experimentation needed for innovation.

VISIT ONLINE RESOURCES FOR:

Learning plan template to track projects + uncertainty.

Intrinsic motivation was about six times more effective than extrinsic incentives in motivating people to complete complex tasks that required creativity.

Financial rewards are not the only way to increase the performance of an individual or team.[70]

Fear of losing is often a more powerful motivator than the promise of winning. Therefore, emotionally intelligent leaders find ways to mitigate the perception that there is something to "lose."

Daniel Kahneman's experiments in motivation showed that when people were offered a chance to accept or reject a gamble, most people refused to take a bet unless the possible payoff was around double the potential loss.[71] In other words, you can offer all the carrots you want, but your employees may end up more motivated by their fear of losing out on the carrot than the possibility of winning it.

Only when we understand intrinsic motivators and long-term goals can we build commitment. If people know they are part of the team and their work is valued, then they become more loyal and committed. Remember, we have to move from *me* to *we* and into *why*. Successful and sustainable motivation is about *why*. An emotionally intelligent leader's job is to learn people's *why*. **Broadly, we can break down and begin to cultivate motivation by looking at six intrinsic motivational drivers.**

THE SIX INTRINSIC MOTIVATORS

 TRADITIONAL

"The Organizers"

KEY MOTIVATOR:
Managing & Organizing
Information

Strengths:

- Devotion to causes they believe in
- Following and implementing procedures
- Influencing others to adopt their systems and methods
- Systematic, structured, and orderly

 UTILITARIAN

"The Doers"

KEY MOTIVATOR:
Taking Action

Strengths:

- Working practically and efficiently
- Resourceful in achieving goals
- Gaining measurable ROI's
- Producing and selling goods and services

THEORETICAL

"The Thinkers"

KEY MOTIVATOR:
Solving & Analyzing
Problems

Strengths:

- Love researching
- Naturally curious
- Excellent problem solvers
- Analyzing and systemizing
- Thinking objectively

AESTHETIC

"The Creators"

KEY MOTIVATOR:
Creating & Exploring

Strengths:

- Noticing form, beauty, and harmony
- Devotion to self-improvement
- Understanding their own and others' emotions well
- Thinking creatively
- Love flexibility

SOCIAL

"The Helpers"

KEY MOTIVATOR:
Helping Others

Strengths:

- Exercising selflessness and generosity
- Seeing the needs of others
- Listening well and valuing others' perspectives
- Investing in worthy causes
- Valuing teamwork and collaboration

INDIVIDUALISTIC

"The Influencers"

KEY MOTIVATOR:
Persuading, Managing,
Leading

Strengths:

- Maximizing their personal accountability
- Ambition in chasing goals
- Competitiveness
- Exercising control over their destiny
- Creating strategic alliances

The Six Drivers of Intrinsic Motivation

7.5

Each of these core motivators refers to what makes people tick, and why they do what they do. Take a moment and read over them carefully.

→ Do you recognize yourself in any of these categories?

→ What about the person you work with the most?

Here's a little more about these motivators:

THEORETICAL

What is it? The desire to learn.
An EQ[3] Approach: Give opportunities for these individuals to learn; provide them with opportunities to problem-solve; when asking for input, give them time to give you research-supported answers; don't ask them to focus on subjective experiences over objective facts.

Unleashing Theoretical:

→ Give them assignments that require them to learn and share that knowledge with others.

→ Get them involved in training or mentoring others.

→   Give them a forum at meetings to go over
specifics and details. They want to share data and
information with others.

UTILITARIAN

*What is it? The desire to see high return on
investments for time, energy, and resources.*

An EQ³ Approach: Ask them to work on projects that
efficiently use systems, time, or materials; provide them
with projects that have tangible results or outcomes;
encourage their resourceful problem-solving skills.

Unleashing Utilitarian:

→   Assign them tasks that can be done quickly. They
like getting a lot of things done in short amounts
of time.

→   They pride themselves in doing the job with
limited resources, so you can take two approaches
here. First, you can give them some tasks that
don't require a lot of resources to succeed–they'll
take pride in making something out of very little.
Second, you can put them in a challenging role
that requires them to perform, and to figure out
how to most efficiently get things done. Recognize
their eye for efficiency.

AESTHETIC

What is it? The desire to create and experience harmony, beauty, and balance.

An EQ³ Approach: Create flexible processes and systems to encourage creativity; respect their desire for balance between their work and home life; find calm, pleasing, and comfortable spaces for them to work in.

Unleashing Aesthetic:

→ Give them opportunities to be creative by allowing them space and time to put their own mark on projects. They might improve it in ways you never considered. Balance this approach with clear expectations around outcomes and timelines as perfectionism may get in the way.

→ Give them flexibility in scheduling their work and home life when appropriate. Show that you value all their priorities.

→ Give them opportunities to improve their work environment—they are highly attuned to the look, feel, and functionality of their environments.

INDIVIDUALISTIC

What is it? The desire to lead, create strategic alliances, and maximize personal accountability.

An EQ³ Approach: Don't limit opportunities for advancement when they are ready and have proved themselves—they particularly value leadership roles; provide recognition for their accomplishments; leverage their motivation to lead and achieve for the good of the group.

Unleashing Individualistic:

→ Let them set the rules, within limits. Ask them to develop a plan, but make sure you provide feedback before they execute their plan.

→ They like outside recognition, so do and say things that show your appreciation. Have career pathing conversations with them regularly to provide feedback, coaching, and assurance that you see a future path for them.

SOCIAL

What is it? The desire to help others.

An EQ³ Approach: Provide opportunities for collaboration and other human interactions; recognize that they will often place higher value on people over tasks; difficult people decisions will be especially hard for them and they may avoid it, so provide support and accountability.

Unleashing Social:

→ Demonstrate the human impact their work has.

→ Ask them to mentor others, get involved in internal training programs, or be a resource for onboarding new hires.

→ Focus on the organization's commitment to its people with opportunities to socialize and build camaraderie.

TRADITIONAL

What is it? The desire to follow a set of principles to guide their life.

An EQ³ Approach: Align their work with projects that are congruent with their core values and provide them with structure, order, and clarity. This motivational style needs significantly more structure and order to be effective than the other styles.

Unleashing Traditional:

→   Give them structure by providing guidelines around a task or project, and clarity on who holds the authority for decisions. Once they are comfortable and familiar with the process, ask for input on process improvements.

→   State clear rules, requirements, and specifications around tasks.

→   They value fairness, so focus on ethics, standards, equality, and inclusiveness.

Leaders inspire motivation through the team environments they create.

As a leader, you can create an environment that unleashes and taps into employee motivation. You can do this through a team and the larger workplace environment.

Here's the truth: **motivation has always been a tricky thing.** Carrots and sticks and external tricks can work in the short term. But leaders make a mistake in thinking that their external application of carrots and sticks makes any lasting difference.

Furthermore, many organizations have focused on employee engagement and default to reward programs, merit pay, or lifestyle perks to attract and retain talent. These are expensive and miss the mark. Employees can't be bullied or bribed to stay.

Traditional thinking about motivation puts it in terms of carrots and sticks, or punishment and reward. New attempts at motivating employees are fancy company retreats or an espresso machine in the breakroom. But thinking about motivation in these terms is dangerous, because it doesn't factor in the complexity of motivation.

According to Gallup engagement surveys, the majority of employees who voluntarily leave a workplace report a poor relationship with their supervisor as the number one contributing factor.[72] Those results are consistent with what my clients are reporting—leaders have not fully cracked the code on employee motivation. Incorporating EQ[3] and creating a trusting environment that motivates employees the right way may stop you from driving employees away.

Within this new way of looking at motivation, engagement is a shared process where leaders cultivate the employee's intrinsic talents. Most leaders lack the tools or training to seed and weed their talent gardens.

7.6 How to Drive Intrinsic Motivation among Your Team

→ List the ingrained organizational sticks that drive behavior in your organization. How is behavior shaped by these punishments?

→ Do you embrace risk or avoid it? Are you motivated by speed or accuracy? What are the advantages? What are the costs?

→ What do your employees hunger for? What are your employees' avoidance strategies? Write them down.

**CHAPTER SUMMARY:
THREE THINGS TO REMEMBER**

→ Traditional thinking about motivation puts it in terms of carrots and sticks, or punishment and reward. Motivation that comes from a threatening environment prompts employees' brains to protect, not perform, innovate, or go above and beyond.

→ Emotionally intelligent leaders know how to engage their employees and unleash their intrinsic motivators based on their individual drivers. Emotionally intelligent leaders connect employees' *whys*–based on their six key motivators–behind their work to their company's greater *why*.

→ Motivation isn't sustained through fear, bonuses, or fancy espresso machines in the breakroom, but through employees staying focused on their *why*.

CHAPTER 8

Take Motivation From *Me* To *We* To *Why*

Bill George, former CEO of Medtronic, one of the world's largest medical technology companies, understood how to use emotional intelligence to move his employees and his company from *me* to *we* to *why*. For instance, he would bring in a patient whose life had been saved by one of the company's medical devices in order to highlight how every employee's work helped to save lives. It was a perfect way to humanize their technology.

Bill would also highlight a standout employee's willingness to go above and beyond by recognizing their work, and connecting it to saving patient lives, in front of the entire organization. By helping employees to see that the technical work they were doing every day with machines had real, human impact, he moved his team from *me* to *we* to *why*. But Bill George will tell you that he wasn't always this emotionally intelligent.

Emotionally intelligent leaders are always thinking about ways to move themselves, their employees, and their companies from *me* to *we* to *why*.

You can move your company from *me* to *we* to *why* by creating an emotionally intelligent environment that provides recognition, strives for clarity, equips and empowers, collaborates and coaches, and operates with transparency and fairness.

8.1 How to Provide Recognition

It's important to offer positive feedback for work done well. Because of how our brains register negative and positive feedback (as I discuss in Chapter 2), aim for a ratio of 5:1 of positive to critical feedback. In the case of Bill George, he knew the strongest positive feedback he could offer was connecting Medtronic's work to the company's purpose – which was to create devices that saved lives.

What Not to Do: Don't wait until the annual performance review to provide feedback. Research indicates that providing feedback on employee performance only once a year is not beneficial to learning. According to James Coan, a PhD neuroscientist at the University of Virginia, our limbic brains are asking two questions all day long: "What's next?" and "How am I doing?"[73] In order to create a culture of safety and trust, leaders should aim to provide feedback to their employees at a minimum, every month.

What to Do: Build recognition into the culture. I worked with a manufacturing client who made a commitment to focus on recognition of employees for one year after their engagement survey revealed that employees didn't feel they received enough recognition. This manufacturing client had some pretty ambitious goals and they knew they couldn't achieve them if their employees didn't feel recognized for their talents and hard work.

So, they implemented recognition across the organization, within the team, and at the individual level. In his town hall meetings, the CEO celebrated company successes by communicating accomplishments, recognizing individuals within the company who had gone above and beyond, and sharing stories about customers that had been impacted by their product and services. Teams were recognized for their efforts and achievements by their managers and CEO, and managers made an effort to recognize employees by having consistent, frequent one-on-ones and providing specific, constructive feedback highlighting the impact they made. The executive team was relieved to find out their efforts paid off. Engagement scores the following year showed an improvement of 22% in the area of recognition. Employees felt valued.

And as for the bottom line? The company was able to meet its ambitious goals.

 8.2 ## How To Deliver More Clarity

Set clear expectations and priorities for employees and teams. This may sound obvious, but how often have you asked for help without being able to articulate exactly what you need? How often has it been hard to decide and communicate what's most important? Have you ever been in a workplace where an employee is expected to know what they're supposed to do or fix, even though no one has taken the time to explain it?

Neglecting to set clear expectations sets employees up to fail.

What Not to Do: Don't assume your employees will know what the priorities are. In an article titled, "No One Knows Your Strategy, Not Even Your Top Leaders," MIT researcher Donald Sull wrote that only "28% of executives and middle managers responsible for executing strategy could list three of their company's strategic priorities."[74]

What to Do: Make it clear and keep it clear. A director at an IT company I worked with, Emily, was failing. After interviewing several team members and diagnosing the problem, I learned that Emily was lacking clarity about her role, expectations, and the kinds of decisions that fell within her authority. Her

VISIT ONLINE RESOURCES FOR:

Tools to show your employees your investment in them.

performance was declining because she didn't fully understand the scope of her job. The stress from this lack of clarity was causing Emily's negative tendencies to surface. I facilitated a meeting with the VP and Emily with the goal of obtaining clarity on Emily's role. A clear and concise document was produced from this meeting with Emily's key accountabilities, the current priorities, and expected outcomes. The VP then used this document in their ongoing one-on-ones as a guide for coaching and accountability. Emily's negative tendencies diminished and her performance increased.

Nearly half of 18-to 24-year-olds listed lack of feedback as one of their biggest frustrations.

74% of 18-to 24-year-olds list ongoing training and education as one of their reasons for staying with an organization.

8.3 How To Empower Your Team

Give your employees training, resources, and autonomy. People sense when you invest in them. So, invest—and then get out of the way.

What Not to Do: Empowerment starts with self-awareness. It means you realize that it's not all about you. Then, you figure out ways to use your leadership to elevate the work of others. For Bill George, he admits this was a hard lesson to learn. During his school days, Bill ran for student government seven times, and lost every time. It wasn't until college that Bill began to learn why. Finally, a group of seniors at Georgia Tech pulled Bill aside and said, "You know, Bill, there's a reason why you're losing these elections and it's because no one wants to follow you because you're not interested in them."

What to Do: Empower to serve. Bill George will admit that his efforts were all about him, his ambitions, and getting ahead.[75] The honest feedback from others was monumental for Bill and was the beginning of self-awareness. It took years, and several jobs in-between, but he says that the feedback on why he was failing— because it was centered on *me*—would influence his decision to bring in Medtronic patient stories that focused on *we* and *why*. A growth mindset includes development, empowerment, and openness. As a leader, you should enable and encourage people to build the right behaviors. They do this through shared language, activities, events, and processes designed to serve others.[76] Bill felt that motivating people to reach their true potential was the path to making an organization truly great. Art Collins, president and COO under Bill, who succeeded him as CEO and chairman, reports that Bill "wasn't a micromanager, and let his talented top managers do their jobs."[77]

You can help your employees reach their potential by speaking their motivational language. Employees react to change differently. EQ³ leaders learn who is who. They know some are more sensitive to rewards and are motivated by opportunities. Others, on the other hand, are much more sensitive to threats and are motivated to protect and guard.

> **STORY: THE SAVVY SOCCER COACH**
>
> One study found that soccer players' performance improved if the coach framed the task to match the players' motivational focus. The shooting coach for a soccer team in Germany, told some players to make three out of five goals and told others to only miss two. Players who were intrinsically motivated by opportunities scored more points when they were asked to gain three goals. Players that were naturally motivated to protect performed better when they were told how many they could lose (two goals), but still be able to protect their team.[78]

Now, take a moment–which do you think you would respond better toward? Depending on your motivation style, it can be strange to think of the other way of motivating. Emotionally intelligent leaders recognize that to empower a team to reach a greater purpose, you must influence each member of the team according to *their* individualized fears and motivations.

How to Collaborate and Coach

Treat your employees like they are your partners. Create an environment in which there is psychological and emotional safety. Make sure your employees know that failure does not equal punishment and if they bring up ideas, big or small, they will be heard. Validate people for more than just the work they produce; get to know them personally and allow them to get to know you in order to build rapport. You'll build trust and they'll come to you when they need help.

What Not to Do: Allowing no room for failure is a surefire way to sabotage innovation. I'm sure most of you are thinking, o*f course, I would never punish an employee for failure.* But when I ask employees how their company approaches failure, I too often hear, "Oh they say it's OK to fail, but it's really not. There are consequences for failing." If employees fear making mistakes, a threat is triggered in their brains. Employees have to *believe and see that* it's OK to fail at times. How people *feel* is predictive of how they will *behave*.

For examples of one-on-one plans, check out our additional resources at: www.thinkaperio.com/eq3book

What to Do: Coach to collaborate. To better help employees fully understand their purposes at work, try one-on-one plans where you connect an employee's work to the larger mission and goals of the organization. Showing how their individual goals impact the organization's strategic priorities answers the question *why* and creates meaning for the employee's day-to-day contributions. Asking the employee where they feel like they can add more value to the strategic priorities is also critical. Feeling like we're part of a team with a larger purpose helps quell the limbic brain that wants to lock down to *protect*. As a result, people feel freer to work together to come up with creative ideas.

When I worked with leaders at a fast-growing advertising firm, we took this approach with a young aspiring leader, Aidan. After meeting with Aidan, we realized that he was unclear about his future with the company. He said he was happy to help, but wasn't sure where exactly his manager wanted him or where he could add the most value. After meeting with his manager to plan his future and create a vision, and coaching to develop skills Aidan would need to achieve this vision, we noticed a shift in him. We measured Aidan's 360 feedback 90 days later, and saw that his team reported a 50% increase in his leadership skills. That's a pretty significant shift perceived by his team in a short amount of time.

An individual development plan itself, as Christine Comaford writes in *Forbes*, "is not simply a potential career path." It is a "commitment from the company to the individual to help them grow." Plans like the ones we made with Aidan consist of three components:

1. Planning the employee's future at their organization (which indicates that they are safe in their role);

2. Creating a vision in which the employee can increase their impact for the group (which indicates that they belong); and

3. Co-creating a way for them to shine even more brightly in their current position (which indicates that they matter).

You do not need to wait for the end of the year or season to start talking about what's next for your employees. You can begin this valuing and motivating process with them today.

 ## 8.5 How to Operate with Transparency and Be Fair

Give your employees the benefit of the doubt, be fair, and keep your promises. Share information about where the company is, disclose the reasoning behind decision-making, and be authentic and vulnerable. **Studies show that management transparency is the** most significant predictor of employee happiness and it boosts creativity in teams.[79] Leaders who practice transparency are seen as more trustworthy and effective.

What Not to Do: Don't guard non-sensitive information and don't make decisions in isolation. When employees feel out of the loop, they experience a 58% drop in perceived group standing. Yep, that's a social threat. When employees feel excluded, their anxiety increases and they become less engaged.

What to Do: Become transparent. When leaders share information, are open about the reasons behind their decisions, and are authentic, research shows that it boosts employee creativity by creating a sense of psychological safety.

Bill George learned a valuable lesson on transparency. When he took over leadership of Honeywell's space and aviation sector he discovered $25 million in overruns that had to be reported. Once it was communicated to shareholders, it spiraled down into negative PR and their stock fell. Bill recognized that he had to keep digging into the issue. After three months, they discovered the problem was even bigger than they first realized. They had more than $450M in overruns. The board of directors and shareholders were upset. They now had a credibility problem.

Bill reflected on how he handled the situation. He realized his mistake. He failed to be fully transparent. He failed to communicate the company's need to dig deeper to determine the full scope of the problem. The overruns would still have created a dip in their stock, but he could have avoided a credibility problem. Bill George learned a valuable insight. In his words: "Maintaining credibility trumps uncertainty every time."[80]

8.6 The Best Leaders Are Meaning-Makers

In the shadow of company restructures, disrupted marketplaces, and our VUCA environment, it's far easier for dysfunctional behavior in ourselves and our employees to emerge. After all, we first established the habits that would be our derailers as a way to cope—and managing disruptive tendencies is easier in simpler conditions.

So what's an emotionally intelligent leader to do?

Emotionally intelligent leaders take themselves, their employees, and their companies from *me* to *we* to *why*.

How?

Be a Meaning-Maker. As leaders, we might be good at sharing financials and other metrics. But it's the stories about the impact we make that are often more motivating to employees. In a VUCA environment, people will search for meaning as a way of trying to understand and make sense of the uncertain world around them.

A meaning-maker is someone who articulates a team's objective in a way that spurs motivation.

Meaning-makers communicate a collective sense of what the group is trying to accomplish.[82] A company's vision should ideally surface from within—and that's where meaning-makers come in. Uncovering and communicating the meaning is what emotionally intelligent leaders do.

Let's go back to Bill George. He wasn't always a meaning-maker. He experienced some of the biggest challenges we face as humans much earlier than many of us: the loss of a parent and the loss of a partner.

When he was 24, his mother died suddenly. He never got the chance to say goodbye, and he was an only child. Bill was left feeling lost.

Eighteen months later, when he was just three weeks from getting married, Bill's fiancée died suddenly from a malignant brain tumor. Bill reflected on this experience, "It was totally unexpected. She was gone and again, I felt very much alone". These experiences would later lead to his understanding to focus on "we" as a leader, but it would take him a while to get there.

Years later, prior to his tenure at Medtronic, Bill found himself on course to becoming CEO at Honeywell, yet he was miserable. "Why am I miserable when I think I'm supposed to be happy?" he wondered. Through conversations with people close to him, it became increasingly obvious that he had made his career at Honeywell about chasing his own ego. He was offcourse because he had been too focused on the idea of becoming the CEO of a global corporation.[83] His *me* story was one of ego, ambition, expectation, and loss. The *me* was all he saw and the *we* had been lost.

Once he had this realization, Bill knew he needed to make a change. Change that would require a lot of humility. Change that would transition him from the *me* and his own ego to the *we*. Bill claimed it took a lot of self-awareness, which is something that he feels most leaders lack.

"Self-awareness is the core of authenticity."[84] It requires humility, learning from experiences you faced earlier in life, and listening to those willing to give you honest feedback."

Over the years, Bill had been approached three separate times about taking the role of president at Medtronic. Each time he said no; his ego would not allow him to consider the move to a significantly smaller organization. After realizing he was pursuing a CEO role at Honeywell for the wrong reasons, he went back to Medtronic and spoke to their founder, Earl Bakken. He realized that it was a company with a mission and values that he could embrace.[85] Bill recalls walking in on his first day. "It just felt like a place where I could be me. I can be alive and I can be who I am and people appreciate who I am. I don't have to be something different than what I am. I can be the authentic me."[86]

Rather than getting caught up in money, fame, and power at Medtronic, Bill continually strove to be what he defined as an "authentic leader" driven by the *why* — purpose, values, and relationships.[87] Bill believes the key to living out these principles is through honest introspection and honest feedback from others. Another way of putting it? An environment where emotional intelligence is front and center.

"Leadership is really about how we empower others, how we inspire them to perform at the top level," Bill says. "So we must make that journey from 'I' to 'We.' We must learn that people are not there to serve us. We are there to serve them. This shifts us from top-down leadership to collaborative leadership."

You know you are making the *me* to *we* to *why* shift when the people you lead begin asking the right questions. Instead of "What's in it for me?" employees ask, "How can we work together to achieve something that matters?"

When the majority of employees show up asking this question, the respect, trust, and purpose the leader cultivated begins to flourish. Can this be created in every organization? Leaders like Bill George, Fred Rogers, and Ben and Jerry had the courage to try. They transformed themselves and those around them. Leaders with enough emotional intelligence to create this kind of environment find that profits flow more easily from a healthy culture.

After 10 years with Bill as CEO, Medtronic's market value soared from $1 billion to $60 billion,[88] transforming Medtronic from a "midsize heart-device maker into one of the world's largest med-tech corporations."[89] Under Bill, Medtronic became Minnesota's most valuable publicly traded company, surpassing 3M Co.[90]

What It All Comes Down To

While there is volatility and uncertainty all around us, there is also opportunity. Honest humility about our strengths and our derailers dramatically improves our ability to influence others. Time spent deepening relationships and inspiring intrinsic motivation unleashes innovation. The habit of intentionally leveraging the *why* in demanding environments transforms employees into partners. The EQ^3 advantage is palpable. It creates an aura of fearlessness and authenticity. Leaders who have it bring people together to make a difference in an indifferent world. In the most challenging environments, the EQ^3 leader is who people will rally around. EQ^3 leaders know that, even in chaos, there are moments of clarity—defining moments that challenge us to call out the best in ourselves and others.

There will always be another storm on the horizon. Defining moments await. My wish for you is that, while others may succumb to temptations and pressures, you will be true to your potential. Complete your journey from *me* through *we* to *why* as you craft a culture of heroes around you. Opportunities are hiding within this VUCA storm. Are you ready to seize them?

CULTIVATING EQ³ WORKPLACES:

What needs should I think about in my workplace environment?

PHYSICAL NEEDS

- Is the workplace physically set up to help employees do their best, most productive work?
- Does our culture support physical needs of employees so they can do their best, most productive work?
  - ⟶ Lunch breaks
  - ⟶ PTO
  - ⟶ Collaboration spaces

SAFETY NEEDS

- Are we managing in a way to reassure employees of their safety - psychologically?
  - ⟶ Clearly communicating expectations
  - ⟶ Recognizing accomplishments
  - ⟶ Encouraging autonomy
  - ⟶ Fostering collaboration & building trust
  - ⟶ Treating employees fairly
- Are we approaching obstacles as opportunities for innovation?

RELATIONAL NEEDS

- Do we have a culture of frequent feedback to eliminate fears & build trust?
- Do managers & leadership exercise open mindset listening?
- Are leaders and employees aware of their derailers and their triggers?

RECOGNITION NEEDS

- Are accomplishments recognized consistently?
- Are we cultivating a growth mindset culture?
- Are we creating a culture where it's ok to fail & learn from mistakes?
- Do employees know why their tasks are important in contributing to larger goals?

MEANING & PURPOSE NEEDS

- Are we motivating employees based on their intrinsic motivators?
- Is our culture and its rituals set up to encourage intrinsic motivators?
- Do employees have a vision for how they can grow their skills and increase their impact?

REFERENCES

Endnotes

1. Raz, Guy, host. "Ben & Jerry's: Ben Cohen And Jerry Greenfield." Audio Blog Post. *How I Built This.* NPR, 20 Nov 2017. https://www.npr.org/2018/01/02/562899429/ben-jerrys-ben-cohen-and-jerry-greenfield

2. Bradberry, Travis, and Jean Greaves. *Emotional Intelligence 2.0.* TalentSmart, 2009. p. 21.

3. Goleman, Daniel. "What Makes a Leader?" *Harvard Business Review,* 2004. https://hbr.org/2004/01/what-makes-a-leader

4. Bradberry, Travis, and Jean Greaves. *Emotional Intelligence 2.0.* TalentSmart, 2009. p. 21.

5. Bradberry, Travis, and Jean Greaves. *Emotional Intelligence 2.0.* TalentSmart, 2009. p. 21.

6. Jensen, Keld. "Intelligence is Overrated: What You Really Need to Succeed." Forbes, 12 April 2012. https://www.forbes.com/sites/keldjensen/2012/04/12/intelligence-is-overrated-what-you-really-need-to-succeed/#6c9ac2d5b6d2.

7. Jensen, Keld. "Intelligence is Overrated: What You Really Need to Succeed." Forbes, 12 April 2012. https://www.forbes.com/sites/keldjensen/2012/04/12/intelligence-is-overrated-what-you-really-need-to-succeed/#6c9ac2d5b6d2.

8. Goleman, Daniel. *Working with Emotional Intelligence.* Bloomsbury Pub Ltd, 1998.

9. Gurchiek, Kathy. "Ben & Jerry's Core Academy Churns Up Skills Development." *Society for Human Resource Management*, 1 Aug 2017. https://www.shrm.org/resourcesandtools/hr-topics/organizational-and-employee-development/pages/ben-and-jerrys-core-academy-churns-up-skills-development.aspx.

10. *Won't You Be My Neighbor?* Directed by Morgan Neville. Tromolo Productions, 2018

11. Goleman, Daniel, et. al. *HBR's 10 Must Reads on Emotional Intelligence*. Harvard Business Review Press, 2015.

12. Daxit, Jay. "How to Create Cultures of Cooperation - A Summit Q&A with Jay Van Bravel." *NeuroLeadership Institute*. https://neuroleadership.com/your-brain-at-work/creating-cultures-of-cooperation-a-qa-with-neuroscientist-jay-van-bavel/

13. Daxit, Jay. "How to Create Cultures of Cooperation - A Summit Q&A with Jay Van Bravel." *NeuroLeadership Institute*. https://neuroleadership.com/your-brain-at-work/creating-cultures-of-cooperation-a-qa-with-neuroscientist-jay-van-bavel/

14. Kahneman, Daniel. *Thinking Fast and Slow*. Farrar, Straus and Giroux, 2011, New York.

15. Morin, Amy. "Five Exercises that Train Your Brain for Happiness and Success." Psychology Today, 21 March 2017. https://www.psychologytoday.com/us/blog/what-mentally-strong-people-dont-do/201703/5-exercises-train-your-brain-happiness-and-success

16. Kahneman, Daniel. *Thinking Fast and Slow*. Farrar, Straus and Giroux, 2011, New York.

17. Sip, Kamila, et al. "Why's it so hard to think effectively about the future?" *Quartz at Work*. https://qz.com/work/1494807/why-its-so-hard-to-think-effectively-about-the-future/

18. Kahneman, Daniel. *Thinking Fast and Slow*. Farrar, Straus and Giroux, 2011, New York.

19. Kahneman, Daniel. *Thinking Fast and Slow*. Farrar, Straus and Giroux, 2011, New York.

20. Rock, David. "Managing the Brain with the Mind." *Strategy+Business*. https://www.strategy-business.com/article/09306?gko=5df7f

21. Coan, James. "Social Baseline Theory: The Social Regulation of Risk and Effort." *Current Opinion in Psychology*. 2015. DOI: 10.1016/j.copsyc.2014.12.021

22. Hsu, DT, et al. "Response of the µ-opioid system to social rejection and acceptance". *University of Michigan*. https://www.nature.com/articles/mp201396

23. Homa, Ken. "All We Really Want: Status, Certainty, Autonomy, Relatedness, and Fairness." *Strategy+Business,* Managing with the Brain in Mind, Issue 56, Autumn 2009. https://homafiles.info/2009/10/20/all-we-really-want-status-certainty-autonomy-relatedness-and-fairness/

24. Hsu, DT, et al. "Response of the µ-opioid system to social rejection and acceptance". *University of Michigan*. https://www.nature.com/articles/mp201396

25. Hanson, Rick. *Buddha's Brain: The Practical Neuroscience of Happiness, Love and Wisdom*. New Harbinger Publications, 2009.

26. Haslam, S. Alexander and Stephen D. Reicher. "Rethinking the psychology of leadership: From personal identity to social identity." *Daedalus,* Vol. 145, Issue 3, Summer 2016. pp. 21-34. https://core.ac.uk/download/pdf/41979575.pdf

27. Rock, David. "SCARF. A Brain-Based Model for Collaborating with and Influencing Others." *The NeuroLeadership Journal, 2008*.

28. Haslam, S. Alexander, et al. *The New Psychology of Leadership: Identity, Influence and Power.* Psychology Press, 2011. http://documents.routledge-interactive.s3.amazonaws.com/9781841696102/Sample_CHPT_9781841696102.pdf.

29. Burklund, Lisa J. et al. "The Common and Distinct Neural Bases of Affect Labeling and Reappraisal in Healthy Adults" *Frontiers in Psychology,* Vol. 5, Issue 221. 24 Mar 2014, doi:10.3389/fpsyg.2014.00221

30. Rheem, Don. *Thrive by Design*. Forbes Books, 2017.

31. Baumeister, Roy et al. "Bad is Stronger Than Good." *Review of General Psychology,* Vol. 5, No. 4, pp. 323-370. DOI: 10.1037//1089-2680.5.4.323

32. Zenger, Jack and Joseph Folkman. "The Ideal Praise to Criticism Ratio. *Harvard Business Review*, 15 March 2013. https://hbr.org/2013/03/the-ideal-praise-to-criticism

33. Wilcox, Laura. "Emotional Intelligence Is No Soft Skill." Harvard University. https://www.extension.harvard.edu/professional-development/blog/emotional-intelligence-no-soft-skill

34. *Wizard of Oz*. Directed by Victor Fleming, performances by Judy Garland, Frank Morgan, and Ray Bolger, Bert Lahr, Jack Haley, Billie Burke, and Margaret Hamilton. Metro-Goldwyn-Mayer, 1939.

35. Rock, David. "SCARF. A Brain-Based Model for Collaborating with and Influencing Others." The NeuroLeadership Journal, 2008.

36. Slocum, David. "Six Creative Leadership Lessons From The Military In An Era of VUCA And COIN". *Forbes*. https://www.forbes.com/sites/berlinschoolofcreativeleadership/2013/10/08/six-creative-leadership-lessons-from-the-military-in-an-era-of-vuca-and-coin/#859ba2a2a5b2.

37. Wolfe, Ira. *Recruiting in the Age of Googlization.* Motivational Press, 2017.

38. Johansen, Bob. *Leaders Make the Future: Ten New Leadership Skills for an Uncertain World*. Berrett-Koehler Publishers, 2012.

39. Johansen, Bob. *Leaders Make the Future: Ten New Leadership Skills for an Uncertain World*. Berrett-Koehler Publishers, 2012.

40. Wisel, Carlye. "Disney's New App Will Make Your Look Forward to Waiting in Line." *Travel and Leisure Magazine*, 1 Aug 2018. https://www.travelandleisure.com/trip-ideas/disney-vacations/play-disney-parks-app

41. de Bono, Edward. Lateral Thinking. *Edward de Bono.* https://www.edwddebono.com/lateral-thinking.

42. Johansen, Bob. *The New Leadership Literacies: Thriving in a Future of Extreme Disruption and Distributed Everything.* Berrett-Koehler Publishers, 2017.

43. Taylor, William. *Practically Radical: Not-So-Crazy Ways to Transform Your Company, Shake Up Your Industry, and Challenge Yourself.* William Morrow Paperbacks, 2012.

44. Salovey, P. & Mayer, J. D. "Emotional intelligence." *Imagination, Cognition, and Personality,* 9, pp. 185-211. doi:0.2190/DUGG-P24E-52WK-6CDG

45. Mitchinson, Adam and Robert Morris. "Learning About Learning Agility." *Center for Creative Leadership.* https://www.ccl.org/wp-content/uploads/2015/04/LearningAgility.pdf

46. Flaum, J.P. and Becky Winkler. "Improve Your Ability to Learn." *Harvard Business Review,* 8 June 2015. https://hbr.org/2015/06/improve-your-ability-to-learn

47. Stone, Linda. "Beyond Simple Multi-Tasking: Continuous Partial Attention." *Linda Stone.* 30 Nov 2009. https://lindastone.net/category/attention/continuous-continuous-partial-attention/

48. de Bono, Edward. *Six Thinking Hats.* Back Bay Books, 1999.

49. Rock, David. "Your Brain at Work." *Google Tech Talks.* 2 Dec 2009. https://www.youtube.com/watch?v=XeJSXfXep4M

50. Baer, Drake. "Always Wear the Same Suit: Obama's Presidential Productivity Secrets." *Fast Company*. 12 Feb. 2014. https://www.fastcompany.com/3026265/always-wear-the-same-suit-obamas-presidential-productivity-secrets

51. Saveri, Andrea and Howard Rheingold. "Rapid Decision Making for Complex Issues: How Technologies of Cooperation Can Help." *Institute for the Future*. http://www.iftf.org/uploads/media/SR-935%20Rapid%20Decision%20Making.pdf

52. Nelson, Eric and Robert Hogan. "Coaching on the Dark Side." *International Coaching Psychology Review*. vol. 4, no. 1, March 2009, p. 9.

53. Nelson, Eric and Robert Hogan. "Coaching on the Dark Side." *International Coaching Psychology Review*. vol. 4, no. 1, March 2009, pp. 9-18.

54. Weir, Kirsten. "Power Play." *Monitor on Psychology,* Vol. 48, No. 4, 2017. https://www.apa.org/monitor/2017/04/power-play

55. Weir, Kirsten. "Power Play." *Monitor on Psychology,* Vol. 48, No. 4, 2017. https://www.apa.org/monitor/2017/04/power-play

56. Weir, Kirsten. "Power Play." *Monitor on Psychology,* Vol. 48, No. 4, 2017. https://www.apa.org/monitor/2017/04/power-play

57. DeCelles, Katherine, et al. "Does Power Corrupt or Enable? When and Why Power Facilitates Self-Interested Behavior." *Journal of Applied Psychology*. Vol. 97, No. 3, 2012, pp. 681-689.

58. "How Your Greatest Strength Can Become Your Greatest Weakness." *Hogan Assessments*. http://www.hoganassessments.com/sites/default/files/Derailers_NL_June_12_Edited.pdf

59. Manzoni, Jean-François and Jean-Louis Barsoux. "Are Your Subordinates Setting You Up to Fail?" *MIT Sloan Management Review*. 1 July 2009. https://sloanreview.mit.edu/article/are-your-subordinates-setting-you-up-to-fail/

60. Eurich, Tasha. *Insight: The Surprising Truth About How Others See Us, How We See Ourselves, and Why the Answers Matter More Than We Think.* Crown Business, 2017.

61. Foreman, Judy. "A Conversation with: Paul Ekman; The 43 Facial Muscles that Reveal Even the Most Fleeting Human Emotions." The New York Times, 5 Aug 2003. https://www.nytimes.com/2003/08/05/health/conversation-with-paul-ekman-43-facial-muscles-that-reveal-even-most-fleeting.html

62. Dweck, Carol. *Mindset: The New Psychology of Success.* Ballantine Books, 2007.

63. Dweck, Carol. *Mindset: The New Psychology of Success.* Ballantine Books, 2007.

64. Saad, Lydia. "The "40-Hour" Workweek Is Actually Longer -- by Seven Hours." Gallup. 29 Aug 2014. https://news.gallup.com/poll/175286/hour-workweek-actually-longer-seven-hours.aspx

65. Kahneman, Daniel. *Thinking Fast and Slow.* Farrar, Straus and Giroux, 2011, New York.

66. Gneezy, Uri and Aldo Rustichini. "A Fine is a Price." *Journal of Legal Studies*, Vol. 29, No. 1, January 2000. Available at SSRN: https://ssrn.com/abstract=180117

67. Sull, Donald and Charles Sull. "With Goals, FAST Beats SMART." *MIT Sloan Management Review.* 5 June 2018. https://sloanreview.mit.edu/article/with-goals-fast-beats-smart/

68. Sull, Donald and Charles Sull. "With Goals, FAST Beats SMART." *MIT Sloan Management Review.* 5 June 2018. https://sloanreview.mit.edu/article/with-goals-fast-beats-smart/

69. Rice, Mark P. et al. "Implementing a Learning Plan to Counter Project Uncertainty." *MIT Sloan Management Review.* 1 Jan 2008. https://sloanreview.mit.edu/article/implementing-a-learning-plan-to-counter-project-uncertainty/

70. Sull, Donald and Charles Sull. "With Goals, FAST Beats SMART." *MIT Sloan Management Review*. 5 June 2018. https://sloanreview. mit.edu/article/with-goals-fast-beats-smart/

71. Kahneman, Daniel. *Thinking Fast and Slow*. Farrar, Straus and Giroux, 2011, New York.

72. *State of the American Workplace*. Gallup Inc., 2018. https://www. gallup.com/workplace/238085/state-american-workplace-report-2017.aspx

73. Rheem, Don. *Thrive By Design: The Neuroscience That Drives High Performance Cultures.* ForbesBooks, 2017. p. 49.

74. Sull, Donald and Charles Sull. "With Goals, FAST Beats SMART." *MIT Sloan Management Review*. https://sloanreview.mit.edu/article/with-goals-fast-beats-smart/

75. "Bill George's "Authentic Leadership': Passion Comes from People's Life Stories. *Knowledge @ Warton*. 28 Mar 2007. http://knowledge.wharton.upenn.edu/article/bill-georges-authentic-leadership-passion-comes-from-peoples-life-stories/

76. Weller, Chris. "We Talked to 20 Orgs About Growth Mindset - Here Are Our 7 Biggest Findings." NeuroLeadership Institute. https://neuroleadership.com/your-brain-at-work/organizational-growth-mindset-findings

77. Rebeck, Gene. "Honors: Bill George." *Twin Cities Business*. 1 July 2017. http://tcbmag.com/honors/articles/2017/2017-minnesota-business-hall-of-fame/bill-george

78. Grant, Heidi and Tory Higgins. "Do You Play to Win - or to Not Lose?" *Harvard Business Review,* Mar 2013. https://hbr.org/2013/03/do-you-play-to-win-or-to-not-lose

79. Han, Yi, et al. "How Leaders' Transparent Behavior Influences Employee Creativity: The Mediating Roles of Psychological

Safety and Ability to Focus Attention." *Journal of Leadership &
Organizational Studies*. Vol. 24, No. 3, 2017.

80. George, Bill. *7 Lessons for Leading in Crisis.* Jossey-Bass, 2009.

81. Cryer, Bruce, Rollin McCraty, and Doc Childre. "Pull the Plug
on Stress," *Harvard Business Review,* July 2003. https://hbr.
org/2003/07/pull-the-plug-on-stress.

82. Raelin, Joe. "Finding Meaning in the Organization." *MIT Sloan
Review*. 1 April 2006. https://sloanreview.mit.edu/article/finding-
meaning-in-the-organization/

83. "Bill George's "Authentic Leadership': Passion Comes from
People's Life Stories. *Knowledge @ Warton*. 28 Mar 2007. http://
knowledge.wharton.upenn.edu/article/bill-georges-authentic-
leadership-passion-comes-from-peoples-life-stories/

84. "Forbes: Discover Your True North." *Bill George*. 4 Sept 2018.
https://www.billgeorge.org/articles/forbes-discover-your-true-
north/

85. "Bill George's "Authentic Leadership': Passion Comes from
People's Life Stories. *Knowledge @ Warton*. 28 Mar 2007. http://
knowledge.wharton.upenn.edu/article/bill-georges-authentic-
leadership-passion-comes-from-peoples-life-stories/

86. "Bill George's "Authentic Leadership': Passion Comes from
People's Life Stories. *Knowledge @ Warton*. 28 Mar 2007. http://
knowledge.wharton.upenn.edu/article/bill-georges-authentic-
leadership-passion-comes-from-peoples-life-stories/

87. "Forbes: Discover Your True North." *Bill George*. 4 Sept 2018.
https://www.billgeorge.org/articles/forbes-discover-your-true-
north/

88. Murray, Alan. "The hierarchical leader is out. The empowering
leader is in." *Fortune*. 3 Aug 2015. outhttp://fortune.
com/2015/08/03/bill-george-leadership-ceos/

89.   Rebeck, Gene. "Honors: Bill George." *Twin Cities Business*. 1 July 2017. http://tcbmag.com/honors/articles/2017/2017-minnesota-business-hall-of-fame/bill-george

90.   "Medtronic CEO Finds Business Starts with Heart." *Bill George*. 18 May 2012. https://www.billgeorge.org/articles/medtronic-ceo-finds-head-for-business-starts-with-heart/

Index

A

Accountability, meeting
 derailers with, 135
Aesthetics in intrinsic
 motivation, 156, 159
Agility, 75–106
 defined, 92
 importance of, 103–104
 increasing your, 91–106
Ambiguity, 77, 86, 91
Analysis, 22
Ark of the Covenant, vii
Authenticity, self-awareness
 as core of, 183
Awareness. *See also* Self-
 awareness

B

Bakken, Earl, 183
Ben and Jerry ice cream,
 vii–viii, xiii, xiv, xviii,
 xix–xx, 185
Blame-shifting, 35–36,
 129–132
 as derailers, 118–119
Blaming of others, 36–37
Brain
 fundamental organizing

principle of, 28
response of, to dilemmas,
 82
scan for social threats, 29
taking of shortcuts, 78–79
thoughts processed by, 23
Brainstem, 21
Brainstorming, 9, 87–88
Buffett, Warren, 93

C

Career advancements,
 emotional intelligence
 and, xii
Carnival game, treating
 workplace as a, 145–149
Carrot and the stick
 approach, 144–145
Change
 elements of, 13–17
 self-recognition in, 14, 18
 social recognition in,
  14–15, 19
Children, emotional distress
 of, 7
Clarity, delivering, 170–172
Coaching, 175–178
Coan, James, 28, 169

Cohen, Ben, viii
Collaboration, 175–178
Collective intelligence, 8
Collins, Art, 174
Comaford, Christine, 177
Commitment, building, 155
Community, xii
Compassion, meeting
    derailers with, 135
Compensation, employee
    goals as basis for, 151–
    155
Complexity, 77, 86, 91
Compliance, 144–145
Conflict avoidance, as
    derailers, 117
Continuous partial
    attention, 95
Control as derailers, 120
Core desires, 7
Creating, 156
Culture, building
    recognition into, 169

D
De Bono, Edward, 85
Derailers, 109, 110–112,
    110–116
  accountability and, 135
  compassion and, 135
  conflict avoidance as, 117

defined, 110
managing and
    overcoming, 140–141
recognizing in others,
    127–128
success and, 112–116
Design structure, 15–16, 19
Dilemma flipping, 84–85
Disney World, facing of
    dilemma of long lines
    at, 84–85
Dweck, Carol, 137
Dysfunctional interpersonal
    behaviors, 115

E
Ekman, Paul, 136
Emotional intelligence
    cubed (EQ³), xi
  asking why in, xiv
  awareness in, 95
  environment in, xi, xvii,
    93–94
  relationships in, xi, xvii,
    94
  self in, xi, xvii, 94–95
Emotions, source of, xvi
Employees
  goals of,, as basis for
    compensation, 151–
    155

providing recognition for, 168–170

recognizing derailers in, 127–128

setting clear expectations and priorities for, 170–171

Empowerment, 172–175

growth mindset and, 173

leadership and, 184

self-awareness and, 173

Environment

appraisal of factors in, 9

changing, 12

creating a better, 49–52

in emotional intelligence cubed (EQ³), xi, xvii, 93–94

perception of, 21–45

recognizing your, 75–88

Expectations, setting clear for employees and teams, 170–171

Exploration, 156

Extrinsic motivation, 149–166

effectiveness of, 153

F

Fairness, 178–179

Fear

overcoming with pauses, 63–68

of rejection, 28

Feedback,, not waiting until performance review for, 169

Fight-or-flight response, 30–34, 44, 62, 75, 95, 100, 115–116

Freaking out, benefits of, 69

G

Galinsky, Adam, 122

George, Bill, 167, 169, 173–174, 179, 181–184, 185

Goldsmith, Marshall, 123, 124

Goleman, Daniel, xvi

Gordon, Evian, 28

Greenfiield, Jerry, vii, viii

Growth mindset, 173

adopting, 137–139

creating, 88

cultivating, 39

H
Haslam, Alex, 34
Higher-level thinking,
	creating space for, 101
Holistic emotional
	intelligence, 6–10, 25,
	70
Human engineering
	personality, xii
Humility, retaining, 92

I
Individualism, as intrinsic
	motivation, 156, 160
Innovation, sabotaging, 175
Institute for the Future, 81,
	103
Intelligence, collective, 8
Intelligent use of emotion,
	xix
Intrinsic motivation, 149–
	166
	aesthetic, 156, 159
	driving among team
		members, 165
	effectiveness of, 153
	individualized, 156, 160
	social, 156, 161
	theoretical, 156, 157–158
	traditional, 156, 162–165
	utilitarian, 156, 158

Introspection in emotional
	intelligence, 2

J
Johansen, Bob, 81, 84, 85
Jones, Indiana, vii
Judgment, 50

K
Kahneman, Daniel, xii–xiii,
	22, 154

L
Lateral thinking, 85
Leaders
	as meaning makers,
		180–181
	practice of empathy by,
		3–4
Leadership, 156
	empowerment and, 184
Learning plans, 152
Limbic brain, xvi, 21, 23, 27,
	37, 58, 59
	decision-making in, 24
	derailers in, 115
	need for control and,
		60–61
	social pain and, 29
	triggering of, 41–42
Losing, fear of, 154

M
Major League Baseball, vii
Meaning and purpose
    needs
    in emotional intelligence
        cubed workplaces,
        188
Meaning-makers
    communication by,
        181–183
    defined, 181
    leaders as, 180–181
Meyer, John D., 91
Micromanagement, 57, 59,
    174
Motivation. *See also*
    Extrinsic motivation;
    Intrinsic motivation
    cause and effect in, 143
    defined, 143
    intrinsic *versus* extrinsic,
        149–151

N
Neuroscience research, 24

O
Obama, Barrack, 102
Open-minded
    management, trust and,
    82

P
Perception-shifting
    strategy, 85
Perfectionism as derailers,
    120–121
Performance review,
    providing feedback
    before, 169
Perspective taking, 8
Persuasion, 156
Physical needs
    in emotional intelligence
        cubed workplaces,
        188
Physical pain, 29
Pizza Hut reading program,
    149–150
Positives, countering
    negatives with, 41–42
Power hunger as derailers,
    121–122
Prefrontal cortex, 21–22, 23,
    25, 33, 116
    discussing, 66–68
    solving, 22, 80–81
    solving and analyzing,
        156
Psychometrics, 119

Q
Questions, asking
      courteous, 53–54

R
Recognition
   building into the culture,
      169
   providing for employees,
      168–170
*Recruiting in the Age of
      Googlization* (Wolfe),
      77
Rejection, fear of, 28
Relationships, 109
   avoidance in, 113–114
   control in, 120
Rock, David, 30
Rogers, Fred, 1–4, 5, 6, 17,
      47, 185

S
Salovey, Peter, 91
SCARF Model, 30
Self-awareness, 4, 43, 86,
      100, 122–126
   authenticity and, 183
   empowerment of, 173
   importance of, 133–136
Self in emotional
      intelligence cubed

(EQ^3), xi, xvii, 94–95
Self recognition, 1, 14
Self-worth, 11
Sequencing of decisions,
      102
Soccer, player performance
      in, 174
Society as intrinsic
      motivation, 156, 161
Squirrel-wrangling scripts,
      136
Stress, emergence of
      derailers in times of, 111
Success, derailers and,
      112–116
Sull, Donald, 171
Sustained motivation, 146

T
Team motivation, 141–165
   compliance and, 144–145
Theoretical intrinsic
      motivation, 156, 157–
      158
Threatening environment,
      motivation and,
      148–149
Threat response, triggering,
      32
Time magazine, vii
Triggers (Goldsmith), 123

Trust, open-minded
     management and, 82

U
Uncertainty in, 77, 86, 91
Utilitarianism as intrinsic
     motivation, 156, 158

V
Volatility, 77, 85, 91
VUCA, 76–80, 110, 134, 188
Vulnerability, retaining, 92

W
Why, asking, in EQ^3
     approach, xiv
The Wizard of Oz, 47
Wolfe, Ira, 77
Won't You Be My Neighbor?,
     1
Workplace, as a carnival
     game, 145–149

Want to dive deeper?

The discoveries I've shared with you in this book are lessons I've learned over the years, but I didn't learn them alone. I am the beneficiary of wisdom passed down from successful leaders and scientists all over the world. These strategies can't be implemented overnight. It takes time to create emotionally intelligent habits.

How do you grow your EQ^3 as a busy leader? Ten minutes a day for 30 days will begin to create the new neural pathways you need to succeed. Download our Month to EQ^3 Mastery to start your journey at

LEARN MORE:

thinkaperio.com/eq3book